SOCCER — John Callaghan
University of Southern California

SWIMMING — Donald L. Gambril
Harvard University

TENNIS, 3RD EDITION — Barry Pelton
University of Houston

VOLLEYBALL — Randy Sandefur
California State University, Long Beach

TOTAL FITNESS FOR MEN — J. Tillman Hall
University of Southern California

TOTAL FITNESS FOR WOMEN — Emilyn A. Sheffield
University of Southern California

SELF DEFENSE — Lynn M. Pacala
Occidental College

3RD EDITION
ARCHERY

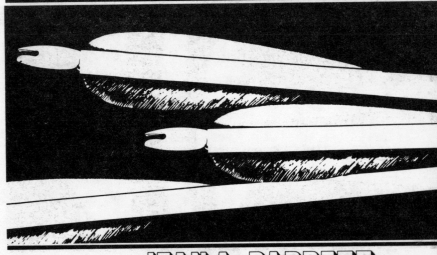

JEAN A. BARRETT
California State University, Fullerton

GOODYEAR PHYSICAL ACTIVITIES SERIES
EDITED BY J. TILLMAN HALL

GOODYEAR PUBLISHING, COMPANY, INC.
Santa Monica, California 90401

Library of Congress Cataloging in Publication Data

Barrett, Jean A
  Archery.

  (Goodyear physical activities series)
  Bibliography: p. 120
  1. Archery. 2. Archery—Coaching. I. Title.
GV1185.B3 1980   799.3'2   79-21037
ISBN 0-87620-038-2

ARCHERY
Jean A. Barrett
Third Edition
Copyright ©1980, 1973, 1969 by
GOODYEAR PUBLISHING COMPANY, INC.
Santa Monica, California 90401

Current printing (last digit):
10 9 8 7 6 5 4 3 2 1

ISBN: 0-87620-038-2
Y-0382-5

Printed in the United States of America

ACKNOWLEDGMENTS

I wish to extend sincere thanks to all those who helped in the preparation of the book. The assistance of Donna Bohannon, Kathy Osburn, and Thomas Lopez who posed for the pictures, and Janice Keasling who prepared the illustrated material, is greatly appreciated. To Marueen C. Rams, who rekindled my interest in archery, a very special thank you. The contributions of the many students in my archery classes cannot go without mention. Contact with each individual has promoted better understanding of the learning process and forced me to delve deeper into the significance of archery as a sport.

CONTENTS

EDITOR'S NOTE

The Goodyear Publishing Company is pleased to publish the third edition of Dr. Jean A. Barrett's popular book, *Archery*. In this new edition she brings the reader the knowledge she has acquired over many years of teaching and coaching this sport. After analyzing the nature of learning, Dr. Barrett has discovered an enjoyable and interesting methodology of teaching people this challenging sport.

The book begins with an interesting commentary on the historical development of one of the world's oldest sports. (It has been estimated that archery was in use 100,000 years ago.)

The author has given special attention to the selection and care of equipment. Archery is no different than other sports; the degree of success in the execution of specific skills has a positive relationship to the maintenance and quality of the equipment.

Dr. Barrett's descriptive style of writing explains the fundamental skills of archery: the techniques of stringing the bow, inserting the arrow, aiming and releasing the arrow. This section on basic skills is followed by a comprehensive analysis of these fundamentals which describes common problems and supplies likely causes and corrections for them.

This third edition of Archery features a new chapter, "Beyond the Fundamentals" which discusses equipment, set up and tuning, technique refinement, and psychological consideration. The chapter "Pointing Up Progress" is an analysis of form and general knowledge providing several self-check lists for recording performance. Additionally, there are several "Performance Checklists" which the learner and instructor may use to review the individual progress in the skill of archery.

Even though target archery is stressed, a variety of sports and games, such as clout shooting, flight shooting, hunting and archery golf add new interest for the student of this ancient, though modern sport. I believe you will agree with me, it's the best archery book on the market.

BIOGRAPHY

Jean A. Barrett is Professor of Physical Education at California State University, Fullerton, where she has held the following administrative posts: department head, director of the teacher education program, and graduate studies advisor. She competed for the Buffalo Archers and currently coaches the Titan Archers Club Team, which shoots in intercollegiate competition.

Ms. Barrett received her Ed.D. degree from the State University of New York, Buffalo, and is listed in *Who's Who in American Women*.

ARCHERY

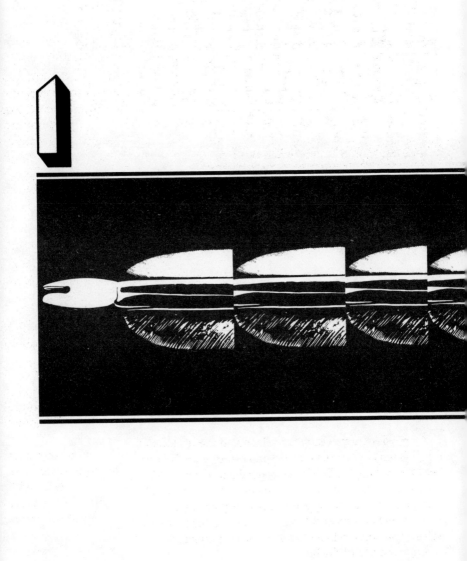

A MEANS TO AN END - AN END IN ITSELF

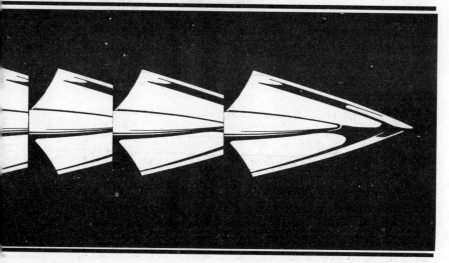

Modern technology has eliminated the utilitarian reasons for developing proficiency with the bow and arrow. The bow, originally used as a weapon for defense or conquest or as a means of securing food, is in present-day society a tool used for participation in recreational and sport activity. To be sure, basic needs still exist in some primitive cultures that are fulfilled through the use of the bow.

BRIEF BACKGROUND

Precisely how and when the bow originated is not known, but it certainly was one of the earliest weapons of man. The bow has been a part of recorded history for more than 50,000 years, but its existence was established well before that time. Archeologists estimate from cave drawings depicting archers that the bow was in use at least 100,000 years ago. For thousands of years, human beings used arrows to protect themselves from wild animals. At the same time, archery skill was an asset in obtaining a food supply. The bow became a symbol of strength and power; it gave man a certain status and advantage in his environment.

Over the centuries archery gained significance in man's life. The bow and arrow became associated with all of his activities and endeavors, all of his moods and emotions. The bow was a weapon of survival, a tool that established man's superiority over animals. With it, direct physical contact with a foe was no longer necessary.

Man's love of music was stimulated by the twang of the bow string. The harp was developed by adding strings to the bow, and archery became further entwined with the culture. In Greek legend, the Amazons demonstrated the ability of women to use the bow as a weapon; they made the bow a weapon of conquest. On the mainland of Greece, the beautifully designed Greek bow became a different symbol, associated with Diana and the hunt and Cupid and love.

With the exception of some Australian tribes, the bow was known to all primitive people throughout the Eastern world. War weapons such as slings and spears became outmoded as the bow and arrow was perfected. According to the Bible, the Israelites and the Egyptians were accomplished archers. The significance of the bow and arrow as a weapon of war can be attested by accounts of world-changing battles. Bows were developed to suit the needs of horsemen as well as foot soldiers. Orientals designed a short bow especially for use on horseback. The English were noted for the use of the long-type bow, while the French adopted and perfected the crossbow. The battles of Hastings, Crecy, and Agincourt, and the Wars of the Roses, were military engagements of historical importance in which the bow played a significant part.

The Greeks and Turks are given credit for the

development of the first composite bows, made of wood, bone, and leather strips. It is interesting to note that it wasn't until 1959 that modern flight shooters broke the distance record credited to an ancient bow. The remarkable Turks were able to cast arrows eight hundred yards with a complex reflex bow that assumed a "C" shape when unstrung. This was quite an accomplishment for the ancients, when you consider they lacked the technical and material advantages of our modern bowyers.

When gunpowder was developed, the value of the bow as a weapon for war or survival began steadily to decline. Firearms eliminated the need to spend many hours becoming proficient in accurately discharging an arrow. However, the bow is still in use by the military: U.S. forces in Vietnam and other areas have found this weapon to be advantageous in special situations. In addition, there are a number of primitive tribes which still depend on the bow for survival.

During the first quarter of the twentieth century, interest in bow hunting was stimulated when Dr. S. Pope shot seventeen African lions with a long bow. Today, hunters try for all types of game, from birds to the grizzly bear. The popularity of bow hunting has caused many states to enact special laws and provide bow seasons in addition to the regular gun-hunting seasons.

DEVELOPMENT AS A SPORT

Henry VIII, an avid English archer who also enjoyed wagering, is credited with the development of archery as a competitive sport. Archery societies or clubs were established in England over 350 years ago. The Toxophilite Society, the Richmond Archers, the Royal Edinborough Archers, and the Finsbury Archers are some of the earliest clubs devoted to shooting. The English tradition has had a great deal of influence on archery as a sport in the United States. Our modern archery tournaments are usually conducted using a "three and three" system based on the English tradition of shooting only three arrows at a time. This practice originated because of the lack of quality arrows available at earlier times. The English officially adopted this procedure in the middle 1900s.

The earliest known archery club in the United States was the United Bowman of Philadelphia. Founded in 1828, it held the first championship tournament in 1829 under rules that are somewhat vague and which do not resemble today's tournament practices. The National Archery Association (NAA) was formed in 1879 and is the national governing body for amateur target competition in the United States. About 1939, a group of Californians interested in bow hunting organized and established the National Field Archery Association. At first, field archery tournaments were restricted to instinctive or bare-bow shooters and attracted many people who enjoyed shooting under conditions that closely represent those of hunting. Today field competition is conducted in two divisions, instinctive (bare bow) and freestyle (sight).

The XX Olympiad held in Munich, Germany, during the late summer of 1972 saw archery included as gold-medal sport. Archery was dropped from the Olympic program after the 1920 games because of a presumed lack of interest in the sport. The International Archery Federation was established in 1931. Its prime objective was to see that archery was put back onto the Olympics. In 1968, due to the efforts of many dedicated people throughout the world, archery was again included as a demonstration activity and subsequently granted gold-medal status at the 1972 meeting of the modern games. This highly significant event lead to an increased interest in archery as an amateur competitive sport, not only in this country but throughout the world.

In 1961, in anticipation of Olympic status, the NAA put forth eligibility rules that conform to the strict Olympic code. Prior to that time there had been considerable confusion as to what constituted amateur standing, and many of the competitions conducted in the United States had been of an open nature, where amateurs and professionals competed together. In addition, some prizes in strictly amateur meets exceeded the value limit acceptable to the Olympic Committee.

Clarification of amateur status by the NAA gave rise to the establishment of the Professional Archers

Association (PAA), an organization that provides competitive opportunities for archers who would not otherwise be able to meet the criteria for amateur standing. Our potential Olympic archers are the young people of today. Unlike many sport skills, in archery it is quite possible to develop a high degree of proficiency in a relatively short time. Proper practice, sufficient competitive experience, and great desire and interest—as well as ability—are the ingredients needed to turn a fair performer into a champion.

In the United States much of the training and preparation of international competitors is accomplished through athletic programs in educational institutions. It is expected that, as archery is added to collegiate programs, future Olympic competitors will be developed by this avenue. Many colleges and universities have established shooting clubs or varsity archery teams for both men and women. Competitions are conducted at local, regional, and national levels, with separate divisions for two-year and four-year institutions. Also, an increasing number of recreation departments are including archery facilities and programs in their planning. The number of participants in all forms of shooting has increased from 1.7 million in 1946 to over 8 million in 1970, and the interest is continually growing. The ancient sport of archery has come of age as a modern sport form.

SOMETHING OF VALUE

By means of modern technology, equipment has been developed that facilitates learning and hastens the acquisition of good shooting technique. This same inventiveness has also led to production of tackle to meet the specialized needs of the many variations of the sport. These factors have contributed to making archery one of the fastest-evolving sports today. There are a number of other features that influence people to engage in this activity, some of which are discussed below.

Archery Is for Everyone

Archery is a pleasurable activity! The various forms of the sport hold appeal for a wide variety of people.

Participants are not limited by age and need not be severely restricted because of physical handicaps. Boys, girls, men, and women have opportunities to participate on an equal basis. Archery is an individual sport. No one else need be present to enjoy the activity. Archery is a family recreational pastime. It is relatively inexpensive and can be enjoyed year around, indoors and outdoors. Archery is a club sport. Clubs provide occasions to meet people, to engage in competition on a formal or informal basis, to work for common goals, and to share interests and experiences. But most of all—archery is a fun activity!

Physical Benefits

It would be incorrect to infer that archery participation is very beneficial in increasing cardiovascular endurance. However, many of the ordinary physiological effects of exercise can be realized to a certain degree. There is a good deal of walking and bending of a type that differs from ordinary work activity. Drawing the bow and holding the anchor position helps to build strength and endurance in shoulder and upper back muscles. Contraction of the abdominals adds strength necessary for maintenance of erect posture. Expansion or stretching of the chest muscles helps to offset fatigue that builds up after sitting for long periods of time—an occupational hazard for college students. Archery helps establish muscular balance and serves to counteract some of the effects of a sedentary way of life.

Emotional Values

Man is a complex creature with many needs and desires. The technological revolution, producing constant changes in man's way of life, adds to the stress and anxiety. Man, in a sense, is a victim of his own intellectual ingenuity. Automation, computers, and assembly lines eliminate many of the former opportunities for personal satisfaction. Pressures and tensions seem to mount to almost unbearable proportions.

Man's image of himself as an individual is daily being chipped away. Man used to take pride in his work.

His ability to start something and see it through to completion gave him a sense of achievement. Work was personally satisfying; it built self-confidence and gave a feeling of control over destiny. Considering our Puritan heritage, it is almost paradoxical that, today, these basic human needs are more readily met through participation in sport and recreational activities.

The ability to handle a bow and arrow competently is personally gratifying; it gives one a sense of pride in one's own abilities and serves to build self-esteem and self-confidence. There is a great deal of satisfaction in sending an arrow exactly where it is aimed. This feeling of accomplishment is enhanced by the knowledge that the work involved in disciplining the mind and body helps one gain control physically and over one's will.

Involvement in a recreational activity, whether it be archery or some other endeavor, provides a means for escape, a chance to "get away from it all" at least for a while. Cares and concerns of the day-to-day world are often seen in clearer perspective once some of our tensions are released. In a manner of speaking, sport tends to free the individual, in that the rules of sport provide the performer with a less complex, more well-defined world where all energies can be directed toward accomplishment of a goal of his own choosing. In the context of sport, man has a chance to truly experience himself.

On Sport and Play

Spontaneous activity of a joyful nature, which has no particular goal as its end, is characteristic of play activity. Play, as opposed to sport, can be broadly defined as carefree, joyful activity, pursued purely in a nonserious manner. The length of time, size, or extent of the play area, number of participants and the like, are subject to change by whim or convenience. Sport, on the other hand, is governed by an elaborate set of rules that define the equipment to be used, the number of performers, the area for conducting the activity, the time period, the method of scoring, and, often, the expected conduct of the participant himself. Sport operates upon a basis of law and order; it could not survive on a basis of expediency.

There are many forms of archery, and each can be pursued as a recreational activity or, in the truest meaning of that word, as sport. The degree of personal involvement, circumstances of participation, and purpose of the activity are factors determining the character of the experience. The potential for understanding one's own nature and the nature of others is present when one becomes involved in archery.

Participation in any sport indicates a willingness to accept the code governing the activity. The performer voluntarily assumes particular responsibilities for his own behavior and makes certain moral and ethical

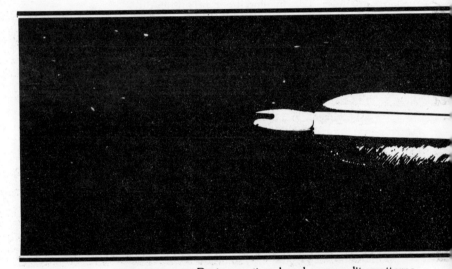

commitments. Basic emotional and personality patterns are brought into sharper focus by behavior in competitive situations.

Sport demands that each individual put forth a sincere effort to produce the best performance of which he is capable. This is a moral commitment. Ability or inability to produce an honest attempt provides insight into the nature of the individual's value system and his character. Archery is not an easy sport to master since there are so many opportunities for human error. Shooting is a challenge that provides an opportunity to explore the depth of commitment to a desired goal. The quantitative score expresses how precisely the archer has focused his materials and abilities, while the manner in which he deals with success or failure presents him with a startlingly clear picture of himself. The rules of sport leave no room for pretense. Alibis or excuses unveil an image of the self that may be more-than-expected or less-than-desired. Fortitude, courage, and persistence in developing one's shooting ability may introduce a more desirable self-image.

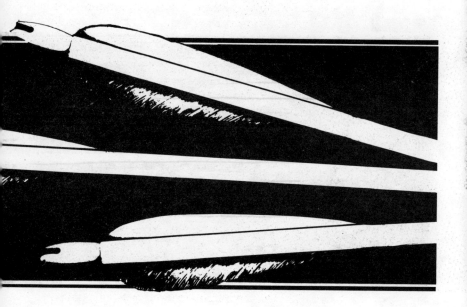

2

FACE UP—SIGHT IN

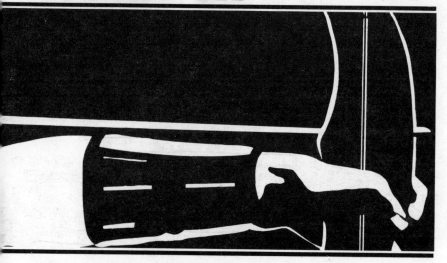

Barring some serious physical handicap or neurological disorder, just about everyone can learn to shoot a bow and arrow proficiently. Many students feel that they are not "good athletes," that they do not possess the qualities associated with good skill performance. If this is the case, the first step toward a mediocre performance has been taken. In effect, a barrier has been erected serving to restrict learning and skill development.

There is a great deal of available information concerned with the acquisition of motor skills. The specialist in the area of motor performance attempts to apply motor-learning principles to the teaching-learning situation. Unfortunately, the average learner is usually oblivious to many of the factors that influence his learning and skill development, often clinging to misconceptions that impede his progress. This chapter deals with some general considerations associated with motor learning and their application to the development of archery skills. The material included is not a complete summary of the information available but rather a sketch of present knowledge based on scientific evidence. The points discussed were chosen because of their particular relevance to learning archery skills. It is felt that if the learner is better informed about the nature of learning, he will have a better understanding of his potential for success.

NATURE OF THE LEARNER

Man is an intelligent, physical, social-emotional being endowed with certain common characteristics of his species. At the same time, he is different from others of his kind in that these traits vary, to a greater or lesser degree, for each individual. Attainment of skill appears to be related to a number of factors. Because the individual is totally involved in any learning experience, certain personal factors are important considerations.

Sex, Build, and Strength

Sex, body build, body type, and strength may influence achievement in some sport skills while not in others. Physiological and anatomical differences between the sexes are particularly relevant in skill acquisition when strength and power are factors. However, many women fail to develop skill to their fullest potential because they assume they are incapable of a high level of performance due to structural and functional differences. Variations in women's attainment levels can often be caused by other things such as lack of social acceptance of women participants in many sport activities and individual motivational level. Sex differences are of little significance in attaining proficiency in archery skills. Archery is a socially acceptable sport form which can be mastered and enjoyed equally by both sexes, young and old alike.

Body build or body type contributes to success in some motor activities. Height and weight, however, appear to have little value in predicting achievement. Potential for performance in archery is not directly related to body proportions, but variables in length of limbs are determinants in the selection of equipment, and do affect distance and aim to some extent. (See Chapter 4.)

Insufficient strength in certain body areas important to a particular movement can be a deterrent to learning and performance. The archer must have adequate strength in many muscles used in the movement if he is to perform well. If this strength is not present, learning will be delayed or inhibited. The individual must possess enough muscle power to draw the bow with ease and comfort to avoid introducing errors into his performance. The following exercises and activities are helpful in building strength in the muscle groups used in the shooting act and in stretching appropriate body areas.

1. Push-ups. Women should use the modified push-ups; men, the regular type.

2. Shoulders stretchers or arm flings. Start with arms extended out to side; bring arms forward so that they cross in front of body; fling or force arms back. This will stretch chest muscles and help tighten back muscles.

3. Lifting light weights. Start with side stride position and bend over at the waist, arms extended. Keeping arms straight, lift light weights by moving the arms sideways to shoulder height. Weights used should become progressively heavier as strength is developed.

4. Toe or floor touches. Hold both feet together and bend over at waist, touching fingertips to floor or toes. The exercise helps to stretch leg tendons and back muscles.

5. Chinning. Grasp the bar with palms toward the face. Pull up until the chin is over the bar and return to hanging position.

6. Simulated draw and hold. Stand with feet comfortably apart. Raise arms so that hands are

close to intended anchor position. The bow hand is turned palm out with the fingers in a bent position; the fingers of the string hand are hooked into the fingers of the other hand. Pull as if the elbows were being forced back and the action of the shoulder, back, and upper arm muscles can be felt.

7. Fingers and arm. (1) Squeeze a small rubber ball with fingers. (2) Start with hand placed palm down on a table. Apply pressure and roll up on fingertips, keeping second and third finger joints straight.

Physical Abilities

Research in the area of motor learning has led to the generalization that skill development is specific for each individual. Factors such as coordination, timing, movement speed, balance, acuity of senses, and kinesthetic sense (feeling) are important in producing a skillful performance, but each of these abilities must be developed for a particular activity. A person who is accomplished in one sport area will not necessarily demonstrate similar competency in other sports. Successful performance in motor tasks depends on a number of things. Prior experience and practice in a wide variety of physical activities, however, may be an aid in learning to perform well. The more experienced and exercised individual may be able to interpret information relative to his performance more quickly than a person who has had limited participation in sports.

Information about body position, distance, direction, force, etc., is constantly being fed to the individual through his senses. So much information is available that the performer must be able to select that which is relevant to the task and disregard those things which are irrelevant. We generally refer to this as "the power of concentration." Awareness of what is important and the capacity to organize and interpret sensory and perceptual information promote appropriate motor activity. Ability to focus on the task at hand and obliviousness to the inappropriate stimuli present is important in archery. Shooting experience and extensive practice in the actual situation are helpful in this respect. Unnecessary distractions, such as tight clothing and inappropriate footwear, should be avoided. Speed of movement is not essential to target shooting; the ability to inhibit movement until the proper moment is a more important consideration.

Social-Emotional Factors

Each person brings his own set of attitudes, values, and needs to the learning situation. How a person feels about himself and the activity he is engaged in will influence his learning. Emotional status, motivation, and level of aspiration are among the factors that explain variations in performance.

Whether tension, stress, and anxiety help or hinder performance depends on the individual and the situation. However, a very high anxiety level or an extremely stressful situation usually hinders performance, particularly when the motor task is complex. Fear builds stress and anxiety and is often introduced into a situation by the performer who feels insecure about his own abilities.

If a learner is not motivated to execute the desired response, he will not learn. Knowledge of results is a form of reinforcement and helps to sustain individual effort. There is always some feedback available in motor skills, and higher levels of performance are reached if there is specific and immediate knowledge of results. Archery has this very important factor built in. The performer immediately knows whether he has hit or missed and forms a picture of his degree of error or accuracy. Quantitative scores provide continuing information about improvement and level of achievement.

The individual affects his own success by the personal goal he sets. If a reasonably lofty objective is envisioned and successfully accomplished, confidence is built and the individual's level of aspiration rises.

Competition

Some individuals feel that competition is not conducive to good performance; scientific literature indicates otherwise. Competition may not prove helpful in the initial learning stages, but performance appears to improve in a competitive atmosphere once the learner has developed some degree of proficiency. The anxiety and stress of a competitive situation for some people may be the factor detrimental to performance rather than the competitive situation itself.

NATURE OF THE TASK

Motor skills are generally classified as fine and gross, depending upon the amount of movement involved. Sport skills fall into the latter category. Gross motor tasks are further defined as discrete or continuous. A continuous skill involves a series of locomotor actions, each of which must occur in a particular order. Discrete tasks embody a single execution and archery can be placed in this classification. Length and type of practices and rate of skill acquisition are other factors that influence learning and performance in archery and should be kept in mind.

Complexity and Form

Shooting a bow and arrow is a relatively simple task in comparison with sport skills such as a tennis forehand drive. The tennis player must be able to judge the speed and distance of an oncoming projectile, position himself properly, and execute a series of movements to successfully return the ball. The archer, on the other hand, is aware of or estimates the distance to the target, which is usually stationary, and executes the act from a static position. He repeats exactly the same basic movements each time he shoots, adjusting only the elevation and lateral position of the bow arm to send his arrows in the intended direction.

The particular form a person uses in executing a skill is an individual matter and is really a way of expressing one's self. Good form is based on scientific and a priori evidence and should be developed. Individual differences, especially in body structure and proportions, may necessitate allowances for several means of execution, but the underlying mechanical and kinesiological principles are still evidenced. The principles related to good form in shooting are discussed in Chapter 5. The learner should strive to understand mechanical, anatomical, and kinesiological principles and how they apply. Initially the basics should be practiced. Then, individual variations, either suggested by the instructor or discovered through experimentation, can be employed.

Learning Rate

The rate of skill acquisition varies with the individual and the particular skill. Early success does not necessarily indicate later achievement. Generally speaking, the initial phase of learning is usually quite rapid. Gradually, even as practice continues, progress slows down to a level of almost no improvement. However, performance and learning are not exactly the same. Learning can be occurring even though the performance does not show improvement in relation to the effort expended. The term "learning plateau" is often used to describe the phenomenon where the performance seems to reach a stalemate or even deteriorate somewhat. Lack of motivation, failure to learn the skill properly, or inattention to the performance are elements that contribute to this slowdown. Effort should be made to analyze and correct the difficulty so that progress can continue. Each individual should allow enough time to perfect his own performance. Keep in mind the fact that the time needed will not be the same for each person. If a "plateau" is reached, the archer must have patience and allow motivation to continue to prevail. Remember, learning may still be taking place even though there is no appreciable improvement in performance. If there is a desire to improve, this intent will lead to better performance.

Practice

Practice may make perfect, but it is more correct to say that practice serves to make permanent. Errors in form or execution may actually be perpetuated if practiced. A number of factors must be taken into consideration if the practice period is to be beneficial. The learner must be aware of, and pay attention to, clues relevant to his performance.

Extended practice periods are valuable to those individuals who demonstrate initial difficulty with the task. Supervision and consistent evaluation aid in obtaining a reliable measure of the benefit of practice sessions. No single method of instruction or practice is appropriate for all skills or every learner. Each learner must be able to ascertain his needs and direct his practice efforts accordingly. At first, it is better to learn the skill as an entity. If a particular aspect of the task appears to be hindering the performance, that part should be practiced so that the specific difficulty can be overcome.

Actual involvement in the setting where the skill is to be used is the best practice. However, picturing the task mentally, thinking through what is to be done, can aid in learning. Some people need more practice than others because of differences in learning rate. The learner should recognize this and arrange sufficient time for practice outside the regular class period if he is to reap the benefits related to skillful participation in a sport activity.

MEANING FOR THE ARCHER

There is nothing like the feeling of accomplishment when the arrow strikes the "bull" or gold of the target. Conversely, continued frustration serves to lessen initiative and desire to perfect shooting skill. The learner can do much to contribute to his own success in archery by evaluating his own motivation, needs, desires, and applying his knowledge about learning motor skills to the particular situation. If a definite goal is kept in mind, there is nothing to stand in the way of reaching it—except the individual himself. The goals must be realistic and yet challenging, with sufficient time allotted for attainment.

The learner must do his own learning. No one can get inside his body and think through or perform an act for him. He alone is responsible for and capable of achieving success. Physical characteristics must be considered in determining form and selecting equipment but these do not necessarily affect the potential for performance. There is no such thing as general motor ability or the "all-around athlete"; each person is capable of performing well, but some people require longer than others to successfully demonstrate an acceptable level of performance.

Level of aspiration, motivation, attitude, and need to achieve are individual variables which affect results.

These factors are as important in learning archery as they are in other athletic endeavors. Adequate instruction and appropriate repetition and practice are necessary to learning, but the final measure of success or failure rests with the beginner himself.

People usually persist in a sport in which they feel they can become adept. The benefits derived from activity are consistent with the effort put forth and the manner in which the task is approached. Believe in yourself and your ability to learn. *FACE UP—SIGHT IN* on your target!

SUGGESTED TASKS FOR THE LEARNER

1. Determine your strength needs. Select a number of developmental exercises and write out a program for yourself that includes a time schedule. Keep a record so that you will be aware of your progress.

2. List your ideas about motor learning prior to reading this chapter as you recall them. Check your list with the information given in the book. Note the differences and similarities.

3. Make a list of the factors affecting performance and analyze how you feel about yourself with regard to these points.

4. Set a definite goal for yourself. What is the *exact* score you desire to attain? Define your level of aspiration.

5. Set up a definite date to achieve the desired score or objective.

6. Develop a written plan for achieving your objective and put it into action. Keep in mind your self-analysis and the factors influencing learning.

7. Keep a record of your progress toward your goal. Record anecdotal notes of your feelings about yourself and your ability to perform after each day of shooting.

8. Try to recall what it felt like to hit the center of the gold for the very first time. How did it compare with other experiences you have had in other areas?

3

PERTINENT ARCHERY TERMS

All areas of endeavor have a specific terminology. The list which follows is not intended to be all-inclusive. The terms selected should help you become familiar with the vocabulary associated with archery and should facilitate communication. As you become more involved with the sport, you will find that your personal vocabulary will expand.

Addressing the target

Standing ready for target shooting with the feet straddling the shooting line.

Anchor

The position at which the string hand is fixed while holding and aiming.

Archery

The art, skill, and practice of shooting with a bow and arrow.

Archery golf

An adaptation of the game of golf, played on a real or simulated golf course, using a bow and arrow.

Arm guard

A device used to protect the bow arm from string abrasions.

Arrow plate

The side of the bow sight window where the arrow rubs as it is drawn, often protected in some manner.

Arrow rest

A projection on the bow above the grip upon which the shaft of the arrow rests.

Back

The side of the bow away from the string.

Backing

Material put on the back of the bow to improve the cast or reinforce the bow.

Belly

The side of the bow facing the string and nearest to the archer.

Blunt

A hard rubber, metal, or plastic tip used for hunting small game.

Bow arm or bow hand

The hand or arm which holds the bow in preparation for and during shooting.

Bow rack

A device, either portable or stationary, designed to hold the bow while it is not being used.

Bow sight

A device, attached to the bow, which the archer uses when aiming.

Bowyer

One who makes bows.

Brace

To string a bow; to prepare a bow for shooting by putting the string into the notches of the bow.

Brace height

The proper distance of the string from the pivot point of the bow; recommended by the manufacturer.

Cant

The slight tilting of the bow where the upper limb is moved to the left or right.

Cast

The speed with which an arrow leaves the bow; the distance a bow can shoot.

Clout

A target flat on the ground which usually measures 48' in diameter.

Cock feather

In modern archery terminology, the "index feather." The feather at right angles to the nock of the arrow. Usually a different color from the other two feathers.

Composite bow

A bow consisting of different layers of materials.

Creeping

The slightly forward movement of a fully drawn arrow before it is released.

Crest

The marking on the arrow, usually composed of one or more colors, which aids in identification.

Dead release

Releasing by forcibly opening or straightening the fingers with the string hand remaining at anchor position. Denotes lack of use of the large muscles of the upper back on the draw.

Double round
A round consisting of two identical single rounds.

Draw
The process of bringing the string back into a position to release an arrow; the distance to which a bow is drawn.

Drift
A deviation of the arrow in flight due to the wind.

Elevation
The height of the bow hand when aiming.

End
Usually six arrows shot in succession or in two groups of three; in field archery, four arrows; in indoor archery, five arrows.

Eye
A loop in the end of the string fitted into the notches of the bow. Same as *loop.*

Face
See *belly.*

Field captain
The male official in charge of a tournament.

Finger tab
Flat piece of leather worn on the string hand to protect the fingers and provide a smooth release.

Fistmele
A term describing the height of the fist with the thumb extended, used in measuring the distance between the bow and the string when the bow is braced, usually a distance of 6 to 7". Most modern bows do not conform to this measurement; see *brace-height.*

Fletching
The feathers or vanes on an arrow.

Flight shooting
The effort to shoot an arrow the farthest distance possible.

Flu-Flu
An arrow with an oversize fletching used in hunting or archery games.

Gap

A method of aiming by estimating the distance between a selected point and the target.

Ground quiver

A receptacle on the ground or floor that holds the arrows the archer is not shooting; often combined with a bow rack.

Grouping

The close clustering of arrows on the target.

Handle

The center part of the bow held by the archer.

Hanging arrow

An arrow which does not penetrate the face of the target sufficiently to hold it in; an arrow which hangs from the target face.

Hen feathers

The two feathers on an arrow not at right angles to the nock.

Hit

Strike on the target in the scoring area.

Hold

Steadily keeping an arrow at full draw before the release.

Keeper

A piece of string, leather, plastic, or other material that holds the string to the nock when the bow is unstrung.

Lady paramount

The female official in charge of a tournament.

Limbs

The portions of the bow above and below the grip and riser section which bend to cast the arrow.

Loop

See *eye*.

Loose

To release the fully drawn bow string.

Mail match

Competition shot in different places, the results of which are forwarded to the tournament director.

Nock

The piece at the end of the arrow, usually made of plastic, which contains the groove that fits on the bow string; the act of placing the arrow on the string.

Nocking point

The point on the string at which the nock of the arrow is placed. Usually marked in some manner.

Notch

The grooves found on the upper and lower tips of the limbs into which the bow string is fitted.

Overdraw

Drawing the arrow until the pile is within the belly of the bow; drawing the bow beyond the required length indicated by the manufacturer for that particular bow.

Perfect end

All arrows shot into the center of the target in one end.

Petticoat

The edge of the target beyond the outside ring; counts as a miss.

Pile

See *point*.

Pinch

To squeeze the nock of the arrow.

Pinsight

A device on the bow used for sighting and aiming.

Plucking

Jerking the drawing hand laterally away from the face on the release.

Point

The metal part of the arrow which pierces the target, often called *pile*.

Point-blank range

The distance at which the point of aim and the center of the target coincide. The distance at which one can aim

the point of the arrow directly at the center of the target
and hit the center of the target.

Point of aim

The point at which one should aim to hit the target; a
mark, used when sighting, upon which the tip of the
arrow rests.

Quiver

A device for holding arrows.

Range

The distance to be shot; the shooting area; an archery
ground, indoors or out.

Range finder

A device for finding an already established point of aim.

Rebound

An arrow that bounces off the scoring area of the target.
It is assigned a value of seven in target archery.

Release

To allow the fingers to slip off the fully drawn string,
sending the arrow on its way.

Round

The name used to indicate shooting a specific number of
arrows at a designated distance or distances.

Self bow

A bow made of one kind of material.

Serving

The wrapping of string around the bow string in the
areas which receive the most wear: the nocking point
and the loops.

Shaft

The main part of the arrow.

Shooting line

The common line straddled by all archers when shooting
from a designated place.

Spine

Refers to an arrow's strength and resiliency.

Stringing
Bracing a bow; securing the string correctly in the notches.

Tab
A protection for the fingers used on the string.

Tackle
An all-inclusive term for archery equipment.

Target captain
The archer at each target who is in charge.

Target face
The front cover of a target, painted with the regulation rings or designs.

Tassel
A piece of fiber or wool yarn used to clean arrows.

Telegraphic match
See *mail match*.

Toxophilite
Lover of archery; one skilled in archery.

Toxophilus
The first book on archery, written by Roger Ascham in 1544.

Trajectory
The path an arrow describes in flight.

Vane
A feather on the arrow, sometimes made of plastic.

Weight
The total pull, measured in pounds, required to draw a bow the length of its arrow; of an arrow, actual weight in grains.

4

TOOLS OF THE TRADE

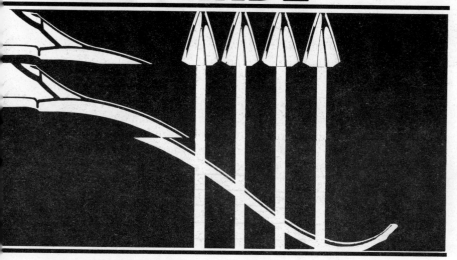

Good equipment, like a good friend, adds to the pleasure of life. Both are a source of enjoyment and both are chosen for their qualities. The choice of a friend is a very personal thing and involves a number of intangibles. Selection of appropriate archery gear is not so complex, but it does require knowledge of the paraphernalia if intelligent decisions are to be made. Equipment is usually provided by the school when archery is a regular program offering. Physical characteristics, such as strength and length of arms, should be considered in an attempt to match the available equipment to each individual archer.

31

Active participation in any sport requires certain basic implements. Archery equipment, called *tackle*, includes bows, arrows, and a number of accessories. Each piece of apparatus is available in several sizes, shapes, and materials as well as in a wide range of prices. (See Figure 4.1.) Variety may be the spice of life, but it can also serve to confuse. The shooter needs to have some realistic criteria in mind when selecting suitable tackle. This chapter deals with equipment from a beginning archer's perspective. In Chapter 6 attention is given to more elaborate tackle and to devices recommended for the serious competitive shooter. Keep in mind that it is not necessary to have the most modern and expensive tackle to learn the fundamentals of shooting.

ESSENTIALS

Arrows

The novice probably thinks of the bow as the most important piece of essential equipment. Obviously, it is impossible to enjoy the sport of archery without an implement to cast the projectile. While the value of a good bow should not be underestimated, many expert shooters give priority to arrow selection. Figure 4.2 shows the various parts of an arrow.

Figure 4.1
Archery tackle and paraphernalia. How do we start to sort it out?

Great care should be taken to select sets that are matched in length, weight, and spine. Inexpensive, poor-quality arrows are not conducive to good scores, no matter how excellent the bow from which they are launched. Matched arrows will fly consistently to the mark unless the archer causes them to do otherwise. Unmatched arrows tend to vary in flight pattern. At short ranges, the use of unmatched arrows may not hamper the beginner, but as the distance from the target increases, the effect of mismatching becomes more evident. Although arrows employed for hunting, flight shooting, target, and other forms of archery are similar in basic structure, certain aspects of design vary.

Arrow Length. Intended use, body structure, and shooting style determine the arrow length suitable for each individual. Ideally, if the arrow is of correct length, the tip will be even with the back of the bow when at full draw. In selecting hunting arrows, the length must allow for extension of the specially designed point beyond the bow. Individual draw length is arrived at in several ways; four of the more common methods are presented below.

1. Yardstick. A yardstick is placed on the center of the breast bone (sternum) and both arms, palms inward, are extended forward without stretching. Arrow length is read at the place the fingertips touch the yardstick. A variation of this technique uses a 30″ arrow marked for every inch from the pile end. This method is serviceable but only approximates the desired length.

2. Arm span. The arms are extended sideways and a tape measure is used to determine the span across

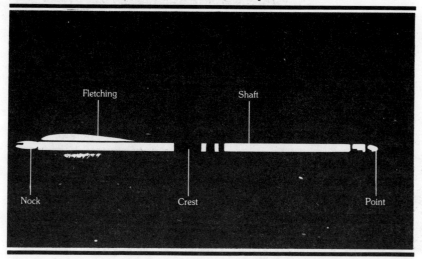

Figure 4.2 *Parts of an arrow.*

the body between the tips of the middle fingers. Arrow length is estimated by calculating 38 percent of the figure obtained or read from a conversion chart, if one is available.

3. Draw measure. The bow is drawn to the preferred anchor. Distance from the string to the back of the bow is measured with a yardstick or tape measure.

4. Bow device. The most accurate means of ascertaining correct arrow length is the bow device. This specially constructed piece of apparatus consists of a calibrated arrow shaft attached to the string of a lightweight bow. The arrow moves back through the guide attached to the bow as the string is brought to the intended anchor. Arrow length is read off at the mark closest to the back of the bow. This method allows for variations in the anchor and body position preferred by the archer and is used by most professional archery shops.

An inexperienced shooter is wise to select arrows that are a little too long (about an inch) until he has established his shooting style. The extra length provides a safety margin in case an overdraw is made (a common occurrence with beginners) and allows for adjustments when experimenting with anchor and stance positions. Matched sets of arrows are all exactly the same in length.

Arrow Weight. Matched arrows weigh within five grains of one another. Superior-grade wooden arrows are available in matched weights, but this cannot be determined by visual examination. Even though wooden shafts are of equal thickness, the density of the material may produce a weight variation. Quality control in the manufacturing of aluminum and fiberglass shafts provides for more accurate matching in arrow weights. While a slight weight variance is not of singular concern in the initial stages of learning, it assumes more importance as the archer develops his ability to send his arrows off in a consistent manner. An arrow's errant flight is not easily detected by sight. Advanced archers often identify arrows with special marks or number decals and systematically record where each shot lands. Inconsistent hits may be due to weight variance or other factors such as improper spine, lack of shaft straightness, or feather damage. Deviation in weight is associated with high and low arrow flight.

Shaft. A good shaft is straight and has a smooth finish without rough spots or edges. Piles, nocks and feathers are firmly attached, and the entire arrow is free from glue deposits. An attractive crest facilitates identification and provides aesthetic appeal.

Wooden-shafted arrows are usually less expensive than those made of other materials and are often purchased in quantity by schools. Norwegian pine is the preferred wood, but Port Oxford cedar, although somewhat less durable, is commonly used. Birch shafts are least expensive but the tendency to warp easily makes purchase a poor long-term investment.

Fiberglass shafts have become extremely popular recently. Characteristics such as lightness, durability, and resistance to warping hastened the adoption of this shaft material by many institutions and individuals. Matched sets of fiberglass arrows are considered to perform better than matched sets of wooden arrows.

The most expensive arrows are made with aluminum shafts and are usually selected by the more serious tournament archer. Aluminum alloys, developed through exhaustive research by manufacturers, allow arrows to be produced with extremely fine tolerances. Metal shafts are not subject to warp but have a tendency to bend if stepped on or upon impact with hard objects. Although original straightness can be restored with the use of specially designed tools or, in some cases, by hand, the bending factor is a consideration in selection.

Spine. Flexibility or stiffness of the arrow's shaft is called *spine*. Arrows matched for spine are within 0.02° of each other in deflection when subjected to measurement on a spine tester. Erratic grouping results unless spine is compatible with the poundage of the bow and the type and weight of the arrow. Proper spine specifications have been regulated by manufacturers.

The archer who has developed uniformity in his technique but fails to have his arrows cluster in a consistent manner should suspect improper arrow spine as a possible cause. Arrows that are too stiff brush the bow on release, resulting in some loss of impetus and deviation in direction. Shafts that are too flexible produce right-left errors as the arrow fails to stabilize in flight.

Fletching. The feathers or vanes at the end of the shaft stabilize the flying arrows. (See Figure 4.3.) Each vane is of the same size, shape, and stiffness on a quality arrow. It is possible for the number of feathers used in the fletch to vary, but the most common arrangement is three. Two feathers of similar color, with an odd-colored *index feather* at right angles to the groove in the arrow's nock, are spaced symmetrically on the shaft. Identical characteristics of curve or straightness are considered in selecting feathers for matched sets of arrows.

The size and shape of the fletching may be altered for special circumstances. A flu-flu fletch is often used for hunting small game because the exaggerated size of the feathers slows the arrow quickly, allowing easy retrieval if the intended target is missed. Plastic vanes are available, although their use is not recommended for the beginning archer.

Points. The tip of the arrow is called the *point or arrowhead*. The primary consideration in selecting a

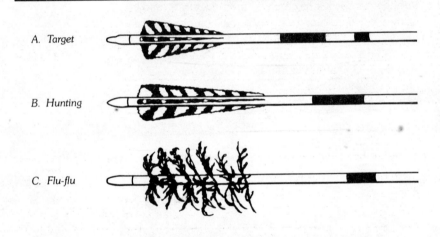

A. Target

B. Hunting

C. Flu-flu

Figure 4.3 Types of fletchings.

particular type of point for an arrow is the intended use of the projectile. Whatever type is selected, care has to be taken to see that it is securely attached to the shaft and correctly aligned. Target points are bullet-shaped or parallel, the latter being preferable. The field point type of arrowhead is constructed to suit the conditions encountered in this form of shooting. Hunting tips are found in many shapes and sizes, and varying according to the kind of game the archer expects to hit. (See Figure 4.4.)

Bows

Bows are constructed of many materials and come in different sizes, shapes, weights, and lengths. Although some bows are multipurpose, selection of a bow is usually made with a primary purpose in mind. Hunting bows are heavier, and often shorter, than target or field archery bows. The competitive target archer, who may send more than two hundred arrows flying toward a stationary target in a day's shooting, would seldom select the same bow as the hunter stalking large game.

Bow design has been greatly influenced by the development of fiberglass, plastics, resins, and strong epoxy adhesives. The traditional wooden long bow used

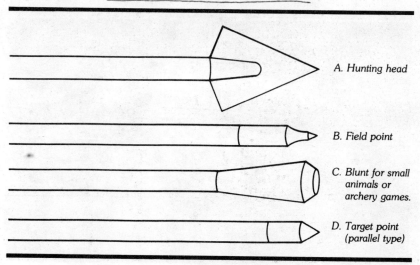

A. Hunting head

B. Field point

C. Blunt for small animals or archery games.

D. Target point (parallel type)

Figure 4.4 *Types of piles or points.*

at the Battle of Hastings, has been replaced by the more efficient composite recurve types. Wood provides the elasticity essential for good *cast*, but it has a tendency to lose its shape over long periods. Solid fiberglass is strong and durable but without the characteristic smoothness of fine wooden bows. Composite bows incorporate the best features of both fiberglass and wood and are considered to be the best available at the present time. Shape, length, weight-in-hand, draw weight, and materials used in construction are factors to consider when purchasing or selecting a bow for personal use.

Long or Straight-Limbed Bows. The long or straight-limbed bow is still commonly used in many schools and camps. Most long bows are designed so that they can be used by left-handed as well as right-handed shooters. If an arrow shelf is not provided, the archer is required to use the upper part of the bow hand as support for the arrow. Unless the handle or grip is specially constructed, the archer is almost forced to use a low wrist or palm hold on the bow. Although some archers prefer the straight-limbed bow, it is considered more difficult to master than the recurve type. Generally speaking, the long bow seems to have many disadvantages; its design does not make it the most

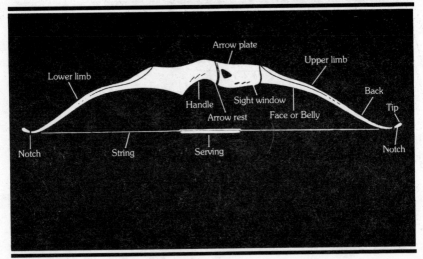

Figure 4.5 Parts of the bow.

efficient or the most durable. The lack of a sight window, which allows for better aiming and a more centered shot, coupled with the uneven stress built up within the limbs during the draw, adds to its negative features.

Recurve Bows. The distinct advantages of the recurve type bow have led to its almost universal adoption by today's archery enthusiasts. All recurves are not the same, however, and some should really not enjoy the distinction of being classified as such. To be considered a true recurve, the string must actually touch the *belly* of the bow for 2″ or 3″ in the area adjacent to the *notches*. If a bow does not have this characteristic, it operates in essentially the same manner as the long bow. If the bow is properly designed, the curves at the extreme ends "open" with the draw, thus providing additional leverage and increasing the potential velocity of the projectile.

The recurve bow is considered to be a "fast bow" because a well-executed recurve sends the arrow off at greater speed than a long bow of the same draw weight. It is estimated that the speed of an arrow fired by a modern target archer is approximately 200 m.p.h. A quality recurve bow also tends to be a "smooth bow"; that is, it does not become noticeably harder to pull or "stack up" as the archer draws through the last few inches to his anchor point. In addition, the form of the handle or riser fits more comfortably in the bow hand. This configuration is conducive to the use of a high or extended wrist when gripping the bow and also aids in achieving a more relaxed bow arm. The cutaway section, called a *sight window*, allows for the inclusion of an arrow shelf or rest and produces a more centered shot.

Recurves can be constructed from a single piece of wood formed by application of heat and pressure. Solid fiberglass recurve bows are popular for school use since they are relatively inexpensive and extremely durable. Composite or laminated bows, made of layers of wood and fiberglass, combine the most desirable features of both materials to produce a strong, durable implement which has good elasticity, retains its shape well, and gives consistent performance.

Continued use of exactly the same bow for each day's shooting is advantageous. Each bow has its own unique shooting characteristics. Two bows may be exactly alike in design, length, and draw weight and still cast the arrows differently. Use of the same equipment allows the individual to become thoroughly acquainted with his tackle.

Bow Length and Weight. Bows are manufactured in lengths from 52″ to 72″; lengths of 64″ to 70″ are favored for target type archery. A longer bow adds weight that is helpful in steadying the bow hand

and aiding in smoothing the release. The added "weight-in-hand" (the actual avoirdupois weight of the bow), however, may produce fatigue if actual shooting is carried on over long periods. The force required to pull a bow to a full draw for given arrow length is called *draw weight*.

Weight-in-hand is important to target shooters since holding a heavy bow may hasten arm fatigue. Draw weight is important to all archers. Unless otherwise specified, most bow weights are given as the number of pounds necessary to pull a 28″ arrow to a full draw. If a shorter arrow is shot, the effort required is correspondingly lessened.

The Archery Manufacturers Organization (AMO) established 28″ as the standard for measuring bow weights. This makes it possible to more precisely determine the bow's actual draw weight for each individual shooter. The procedure involves calculating the difference between individual draw length and 28″. The draw weight marked on the bow is divided by 20 (carried to two decimal places) and this in turn is multiplied by the difference just calculated. The result is added to or subtracted from the marked bow weight to produce the actual draw weight. For example, if an archer is shooting a 25″ arrow from a 30-lb. bow, the actual draw weight would be 25.5 lbs:

$$30 \div 20 = 1.5 \times (28 - 25) = 4.5$$
$$30 - 4.5 = 25.5$$

It is logical to assume that scoring effectiveness is enhanced with use of a heavier bow. The added velocity allows a flatter trajectory. This factor becomes increasingly important as the distance from the target becomes greater. However, while logic might dictate that doubling the draw weight increases the arrow velocity accordingly, research shows that a 100 percent increase in draw weight produces, at best, a 25 percent increase in arrow speed.

Individual muscle strength is of primary importance in bow-weight determination. In their zeal to score well, many archers (particularly beginners) have a tendency to "overbow" themselves. The novice is wise to select a fairly light bow, one that he can draw easily and shoot comfortably. Development of proper form is often sacrificed to bad habits when compensating for lack of sufficient muscular strength. Hunching of the forward shoulder or locking of the bow arm is symptomatic of a bow that is too strong for the archer. Since the upper back muscles, which do most of the work during the draw, are not usually developed to the extent needed at the onset of shooting, it is important to start with a light bow. Increases in bow weight are made gradually, about 1 to 3 pounds at a time, and only as muscular strength develops through use.

Arm Guards

The arm guard could be considered an accessory, since it is not absolutely essential to the shooting act (see Figure 4.6). However, the protection it provides for the bow arm is essential if good form is to be developed. The arm guard is worn below the elbow, near the wrist of the bow arm. Prudent use of this plastic or leather shield prevents painful bruises that result if the string strikes the area. The added protection builds confidence and promotes consistent form. Failure to cover the arm properly could lead to flinching or other detrimental habits.

Finger Tabs or Gloves

The fingers of the string hand are covered with finger tabs or specially designed shooting gloves. Friction between the fingers and the bow string can produce sores or blisters when shooting for prolonged periods. Tabs or gloves protect the areas subject to hurt and aid in developing a smooth, consistent release. Many novice archers experience difficulty in adjusting to the use of finger tabs or gloves and tend to disregard their importance. Careful attention to proper fit and a little patience is all that is necessary to overcome any initial discomfort.

ACCESSORIES

Quivers

Metal ground quivers which hold the arrows upright and provide a rest for the bow when not in use are desirable pieces of tackle. Most schools provide a ground quiver and some institutions also issue a hip or belt receptacle for holding arrows. Other types of quivers fit across the back, on the leg, or attach to the bow itself. (See Figure 4.7.)

Sights

Sights—mechanical devices secured to the bow—aid the archer in aiming his shots. (See Figure 4.8.) The variety of sights available is almost limitless. Each sight is constructed so that adjustments can be made for bow elevation and windage (right-left). Simple sights can be made from inexpensive materials such as cork, self-adhesive weather stripping, tongue depressors,

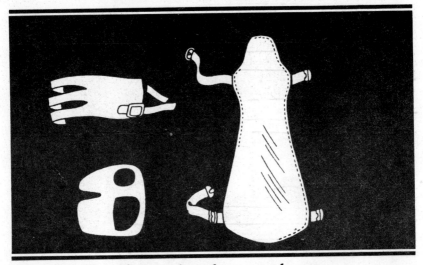

Figure 4.6 *Glove, finger tab, and arm guard.*

and large bead-head dressmaker straight pins. A strip of material is attached to the back or belly of the bow and a pin is inserted on the arrow side to serve as the post. The pin is moved up or down and in or out as needed to correct distance and directional errors.

Other Accessories

Additional accessories serve a number of different functions. A bow case protects the bow during storage and can be purchased or easily made from a piece of flannel material. Tackle boxes are convenient for storage and transporting arrows and other shooting equipment. Chest guards, cleaning tassels, finger slings, string keepers, bow-tip protectors, bow strings, powder dispensers, anchor locks, "kissing" buttons, and mechanical devices that indicate when exact draw length is reached are some of the many supplemental pieces of gear. As interest in active participation grows, so usually does the list of tackle the archer feels is necessary for maximum enjoyment.

CARE OF EQUIPMENT

It is relatively expensive for a school to provide good basic archery tackle. A conscientious instructor should

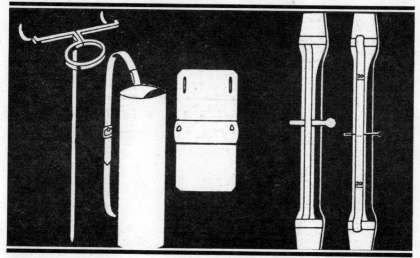

Figure 4.7 *Quivers.* **Figure 4.8** *Sights.*

attempt to secure the best possible equipment with the money available. He knows that good tackle facilitates learning and adds to the enjoyment of the participant. Whether the archer has his own equipment or is using tackle provided by an institution, attention to proper care and repair will significantly increase its useful life and provide a margin of safety. Several pertinent points are listed here.

Bows

1. Brace the bows correctly. (Proper procedure is described in the following chapter.)

2. Unstring the bows when not in use. Some bows will take a set if stored in a braced position; others are not affected.

3. Bows should be suspended vertically, or placed horizontally across pegs, in a cool area that has some degree of humidity.

4. Storage in a case protects the bow from scratches and prevents excess moisture from accumulating.

5. Periodic applications of quality furniture or floor wax will protect the bow's finish. Use of beeswax on the string and paraffin on the servings will minimize fraying. Frayed strings should always be replaced.

6. Bows should not be overdrawn or the string released without an arrow.

7. Bows should not be dropped or laid on the ground to prevent damage by being stepped on or affected by residual moisture.

8. Bows should be "warmed up" before actual use by drawing several times and letting down easily.

9. Bows should be checked for proper brace height at periodic intervals.

Arrows

1. Arrows should be retrieved and carried by the shaft and not by the feathers.

2. Arrows should be stored in racks or in specially designed cases.

3. Arrows should be checked for damage and wiped clean after each end. Cracked or splintered arrows should be destroyed immediately to prevent possible injury by use.

4. Replacement of loose or damaged piles, nocks, and fletchings is essential for safety as well as accuracy.

5. Application of wax to the shaft prolongs the life of the finish.

SUGGESTED TASKS FOR THE LEARNER

1. Check your archery vocabulary by naming and identifying the various parts of the bow and arrow.

2. Measure yourself for arrow length using at least two of the methods described. Record the length indicated by each method. Repeat the procedure after several weeks. Is there a difference?

3. Draw bows of several different weights and note the weight most comfortable for you at this time. Repeat the procedure after several weeks of shooting.

4. Calculate or estimate the force you exert when drawing a bow of a given weight for your arrow length.

5. Determine whether or not your set of arrows is matched. Record or list the points of similarity and/or variation. (NOTE: Most schools do not own spine testers or arrow scales. The instructor can usually provide information about the spine and weight of arrows. The more curious or creative student may seek ways of applying knowledge from scientific disciplines to the solution of the problem.)

6. Shoot bows of different weights and design. Note the differences in arrow speed and trajectory for shots at given distances.

7. Shoot arrows of different spine and weight from the same bow. Attempt to determine which arrows are most compatible with that bow.

8. Find out how the brace height is measured for your particular bow, and check the bow for correct string distance. Make any necessary adjustments in string length.

9. Check your understanding of archery terminology used in the text by writing out definitions and comparing these with the definitions given in Chapter 3.

10. List the features you would look for if you were considering the purchase of equipment for your own personal use.

11. Describe how you would care for your own personal equipment.

12. Replace the nock, feathers, and/or point of an arrow.

5

THE FUNDAMENTALS

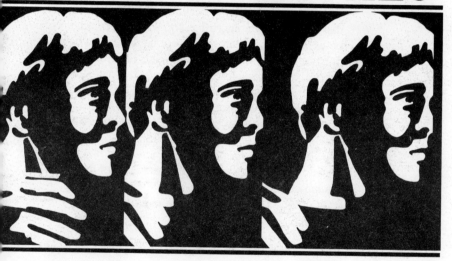

Some archers have developed distinct and unique ways of shooting. It is often possible to identify an individual merely by watching his performance. Factors that influence shooting style include personal preference, physical characteristics, equipment design, and advocacy of a particular theory of shooting. Whatever the reason, the ability to produce a successful performance is based upon familiarity with the tackle and a thorough understanding of the principles governing its use.

Power, necessary to hurl any missile, must be provided in some manner. The bow is given the needed potential energy by pulling on the string, causing the limbs to assume an unnatural position. As the string is released, the limbs move forward, supplying force to the arrow. Concisely stated, shooting an arrow involves pulling the bow string and letting it go! The entire process is simplicity itself, or so it seems. Closer scrutiny reveals a more complex operation. Certain prerequisite acts are performed before the arrow is placed on the string. Other movements precede the draw and follow the release. The basic process is repeated precisely and consistently to obtain desired results.

PREPARING THE BOW

The bow and string should be checked before each day's shooting. Faulty strings should be replaced, and bows in need of repair should not be used. The bow must be *braced,* or strung, before it is ready for use. Bracing increases tension in the limbs by forcing them to assume a greater bend than normal. Stringing is accomplished by a proper application of force to produce the necessary leverage. Some schools have bracing devices that produce mechanical advantage and allow bows to be strung with a minimum of physical effort. Such devices prolong the useful life of the equipment and are recommended. Manual bracing is accomplished by either the push-pull or step-through methods.

Mechanical Bracing

The bow stringer is a relatively inexpensive device consisting of a strong cord with a small leather or plastic cup at one end and a triangular piece of plastic or a cup at the other end. The instrument is attached to the bow and the cord is held down with the foot. The archer pulls upward on the grip, which bends the limbs evenly and proceeds to slip the bow string into the upper notch. (See Figure 5.1.) Care should be taken to see that the bow string is properly aligned and that the ends of the stringer are in the center of the bow before execution. This stringing method is preferred for all types of bows; if a stringer is not available, however, the bow can be braced manually.

Push-Pull Method

Most manufacturers recommend the push-pull method for both straight-limbed and recurve bows. The lower limb is immobilized by placing it against the instep (inside) of the foot. One hand pulls the center of the bow outward while the other hand simultaneously forces the upper limb downward. Once sufficient bend has been obtained, the fingers work the loop of the string into the upper notch. Figure 5.2 illustrates the position and means of applying pressure.

Summary of the Push-Pull Method

1. Check to see that the string is correctly seated in the notch of the lower limb.
2. Assume a comfortable stance with the feet apart.
3. Place the lower end of the bow, back up, against the instep of the foot. Take care to see that the tip is not resting on the ground.
4. Grasp the handle of the bow with the hand on the same side as the foot used to steady the lower limb.
5. Place the palm area of the free hand on the upper limb so that the fingers are in contact with the loop of the string. The thumb and index fingers should be free to manipulate the string.
6. Apply a pulling force with the lower hand as the upper hand presses down on the upper limb.
7. Work the loop of the string into the upper notch with the fingers once the bow has sufficient bend.
8. Check to see that both of the loops are properly secured in the notches and the string aligned with the bow. Be sure to hold the bow well away from the face and body.

Step-Through Method

The step-through method is used with heavier bows or when the archer lacks sufficient strength to use other means. The lower limb is stabilized by placing the back of the bow across the ankle area. The other leg is lifted through the space between the string and the belly of the bow. The bow moves to a position behind the body

Figure 5.1 *Using the bow stringer.*

so that the handle, or riser, rests high on the rear of the upper thigh. The bow is bent by applying force in a forward direction and the string slipped into the notch with the free hand. (See Figure 5.3.)

Care must be taken with this method, as there is extra stress on the lower limb and incorrect execution could result in a damaged bow. It is recommended that the heel of the stabilizing leg be raised off the ground slightly, this is helpful in preventing torquing or twisting of the limb.

Summary of Step-Through Bracing

1. Check the lower nock for proper string seating.

Figure 5.2 Push-pull bracing. Pull with the lower hand while exerting downward force with the heel of the upper hand. Use thumb and forefinger to work loops into notch.

Figure 5.3 Step-through method. Use the leg as a fulcrum; bend upper limb by pushing forward.

2. Assume a comfortable upright stance.

3. Place the back of the lower limb across the ankle of one foot so that the belly of the bow is away from the body.

4. Step the other leg through the area between the belly of the bow and the string.

5. Move the bow to a position behind the stepping leg so that the handle or riser rests high behind the thigh.

6. Raise the heel of the supporting foot slightly to aid in preventing torque or twisting of the bow limbs.

7. Bend the upper limb forward with one hand and move the loop of the string into the notch with the other hand.

8. Check both notches for proper string insertion and alignment.

Safety

Once the bow limbs are bent they possess potential energy. If the string has not been placed in the notches correctly, the force could be released unexpectedly. Examine the strings, seeing that the loops are placed in the right way. The bow should be held well away from the face in such a way that the limbs will not contact any part of the face or body if they should suddenly slip free. Remember, bow tips are rather pointed, so a little care will avoid a serious or painful injury!

THE SHOOTING ACT

Shooting should be thought of and practiced as an integrated whole. However, an understanding of the interrelatedness of each of the subsequent parts helps in analyzing performance. Each part affects the end result in some significant manner. At times it is necessary to practice a particular aspect of the total act in correcting performance; whenever this happens some relearning takes place as the parts are again put together.

The archer should strive to arrive at a definite pattern in reaching for the arrow, placing it on the string, raising the bow arm, drawing, aiming, holding, and releasing the string. If the rhythm is broken at any time, it is better to "let down" and start over than to try to adjust along the way.

The procedure closely resembles the ritual used by many golfers as they prepare to hit the ball: the distance to the green is estimated; the club selected; the feet aligned; the grip checked; the body and foot positions again observed; the waggle performed; and then the ball hit. The whole process is repeated in the same sequence and time structure every time a shot is made. Observe professional golfers on television sometime; you can practically count out the beat. This sytematic approach helps to establish the feeling that everything is right. A definite established procedure provides feedback and allows detection of possible errors before they become misses at the target.

Stance

The initial body and foot position, called the *stance*, is important because it produces the most effective posture

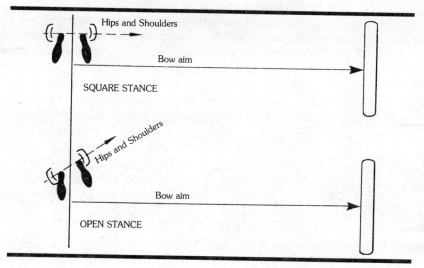

Figure 5.4 *Stance.*

for applying a "sideways" force. The body assumes a balanced position that helps to steady the bow arm during the draw and release. Either a square or open stance can be used to start with. (See Figure 5.4.) It is possible to shoot with a closed stance, but this is not recommended in the initial stages of learning. In the more traditional square stance, the feet straddle the shooting line so that an imaginary line extended across the toes points to the center of the target. The open stance is accomplished by drawing the forward foot back about 4" to 6" from the square position. If the open stance is used, the hips and shoulders must also turn so that they are in line with the toes. In target archery the hips and shoulders may point to the target next to the one used for shooting when the feet are in the open position. Either stance requires an evenly balanced, upright posture with the head turned so that it is facing the intended hitting area. The open stance moves the bow arm away from the string a bit and is helpful in building a beginning archer's confidence. Once the stance position is determined it should remain the same each and every time an arrow is nocked, drawn, and released. After some shooting experience, experimentation with different foot positions and weight distributions aids in establishing the most effective individual style. In some cases, the instructor may recommend changes based on certain physical characteristics or to help compensate for subtle errors in other parts of the form.

Grip

To some extent, design characteristics of the handle affect the manner in which the bow is held. Most modern bows have a pistol type of configuration in the handle, which is helpful in developing a good holding position. While variations in hand position are permissible, two means of holding the bow are more common than others: the high wrist (or extended) position and the low wrist (or flexed) position (see Figure 5.5).

To achieve the high, or extended, wrist position, "shake hands" with the bow so that it rests in the V formed by the thumb and index finger. The fingers are relatively loose and the bow is not actually gripped but braced in the groove so that the wrist is slightly above or directly behind the hand. The arm is fully extended, with the forward shoulder and elbow down and rotated back slightly. If the bow arm is in the correct position, flexion of the elbow will cause the lower arm to move directly in toward the body like a door swinging inward. If the arm is incorrectly positioned, the bow will move diagonally upward or downward, depending on the shoulder and elbow position. (See Figures 5.6 and 5.7.) To avoid dropping the bow at release, the fingers of the bow hand are pointed slightly downward and light pressure is applied to the sides of the bow by the thumb and index finger. Some people have the tips of the thumb and index finger touching as they encircle the bow. A finger sling, which attaches to the index finger and thumb of the bow hand and extends across the back of the bow, is often employed. The device enables the archer to keep the bow fingers relaxed and keeps the bow from falling to the ground on the release and follow-through.

In the low wrist position the bow is braced against the fleshy part of the palm with the wrist slightly below the upper part of the hand. Pressure is felt along the lifeline below the base of the thumb. Many people use this grip successfully and beginners seem to feel more comfortable with it. However, the grip makes it easy to elevate the

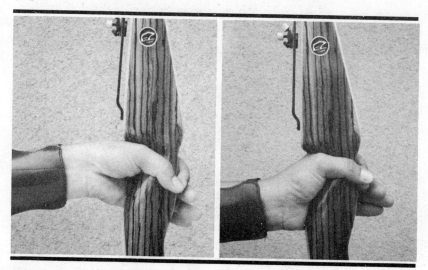

Figure 5.5 Grip: high and low wrist.

bow shoulder and straighten the arm, so care should be exercised to see that the arm and shoulder are in the correct position.

Failure to achieve a good grip and proper bow-arm alignment will result in serious shooting errors. The slightest movement of the arm will cause the arrow to miss the intended impact area by several inches or even feet, depending on the distance from the target. Painful slaps or bruises result when the string hits the bow arm, and this can seriously affect the archer's confidence. Care should be exercised to see that the wrist is correctly aligned behind the hand (not rotated inward or outward) and that the elbow is not locked or stiff.

Nocking

There are a number of ways to place the arrow on the string. Some people grasp the end of the nock, others hold the arrow by its shaft. The bow is held in as vertical a position as possible so as not to interfere with other shooters. Two things should be kept in mind when nocking the arrow. First, place the arrow in exactly the same place on the string each time. Second, place the index feather so that it is away from the bow. At first the arrow is nocked at a 90° angle with the string. But as

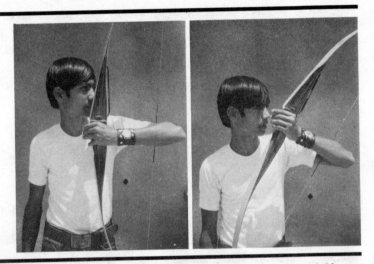

Figure 5.6 Check for proper arm and shoulder positioning. If arm and shoulder are correct, the bow will swing into the body when the elbow is bent.
Figure 5.7 If arm and shoulder position is faulty, the bow will move differently when the elbow is bent.

shooting experience progresses, a nocking point ⅛" to ¼" above the perpendicular is used. A nocking point on the string helps to ensure replication of arrow placement. A piece of masking tape can be substituted if the nocking point has not been served (wound). There are a number of commercially manufactured nocking points available which are easily fixed on the string. The arrow is usually nocked below, not on, the nocking indicator. (See Figure 5.8.)

Grasping the String

Once the nock of the arrow is seated on the serving, the three string fingers are placed on the string so that the index finger rests above the arrow with the two other fingers below. Either the "shallow" or "deep" hook position is used. The term *hook* refers to the position of the fingers, not the position of the hand itself. The shallow hook is the one most commonly taught. The string is placed in such a position that it rests just above or in the groove of the first joint, not on the very tips of

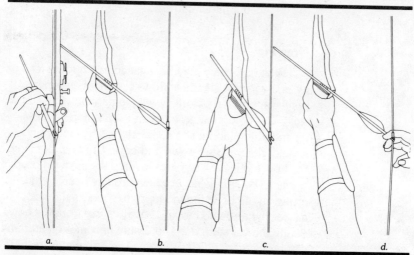

a.   b.   c.   d.

Figure 5.8 Nocking the arrow and finger position on string.
a) Hold bow as vertical as possible and place the nock on the string.
b) Arrow is positioned below nocking point on the string, index feather is away from bow, note nocking point.
c) The forefinger can be used to hold the arrow against the bow until it is drawn to anchor position.
d) Finger position. Start with the fingers slightly apart from the arrow, as the string is drawn back the fingers tend to compress.

the fingers. The knuckles are not bent; the back of the hand is flat and in line with the lower arm; the thumb and little fingers are in toward the palm.

The deep hook differs from the shallow in that the string is allowed to rest between the first and second finger joints. The deep hook is often easier for beginners to use and is not really disadvantageous in perfecting a smooth release. Experimentation with the deep hook will demonstrate that a smooth release is possible once the archer learns to simply relax his fingers.

Both grasps require that the thumb and little finger be moved toward the palm so that they are out of the way. Touching the tip of the little finger and thumb together may prove helpful. The hand position resembles that used in the Boy Scout salute. Whichever string finger position produces the best release is the one to use. The arrow is not squeezed or gripped between the fingers but rather caressed.

Drawing

While the draw may be initiated in a number of ways, beginners should learn to assume the proper bow-arm position before developing an individual draw style. The bow is raised to a vertical position with the extended arm about shoulder height. The elbow and shoulder are rotated down and back. *Canting,* or tilting, the bow slightly at first helps to keep the arrow in proper position. Beginners usually have trouble keeping the arrow on the bow; the tendency to squeeze the nock causes the arrow to move sideways away from the bow. As the draw is started, this pressure becomes greater and can prove to be a real problem. The arrow must rest lightly between the fingers; in fact, it is a good idea to move the upper finger slightly away from the arrow. The index finger of the bow hand can be used to steady the arrow during the draw but is removed when the anchor position is reached.

The forward shoulder position is often overlooked. A poor shoulder position is not always evident until the string is actually started back. Hunching of the bow shoulder is indicative of equipment that is too strong for the archer. In such cases a lighter bow should be used until sufficient strength is attained to handle the equipment. Once the bow arm is in proper position, the string is drawn back by the upper arm, back, and upper shoulder muscles (see Figure 5.9). The fingers of the hand merely act as hooks and do not supply force for the draw. The string is moved back in a smooth and deliberate manner. Taking a deep breath, in coordination with the pull itself, during the drawing phase seems to assist some people. Think of moving the scapula or wings of the back together as if to pinch or hold something between the shoulder blades.

The idea of a perfectly straight line extending from the tip of the arrow, down its shaft, along the back of the hand and lower arm to the elbow seems to be firmly established in the literature on shooting technique. Observation shows that this straight line does not usually

Figure 5.9 *Archer at full draw, using an open stance.*

exist. If the proper muscles are used, the tip of the drawing elbow will be slightly above the arrow.

Anchor

It is extremely important that the arrow be drawn exactly the same distance each time. The drawn bow can be likened to the powder charge in a bullet: if the powder charge in two bullets is different, they will not fly in exactly the same manner. To have a consistent propelling force for the arrow, the arm position and the anchor point must be the same for each arrow shot.

Once this is accomplished, aiming becomes the variable in which adjustments are made for distance and direction. If the arrow is not drawn back to the same point each time, the potential velocity is increased or decreased, depending upon the variation in draw length. Errors of this nature become more evident as the distance from the target increases.

Anchor positions are generally classified as high and low (see Figure 5.10). One high anchor has the tip of the index finger drawn to the corner of the sighting eye. This gives the feeling of sighting almost directly along the shaft of the arrow to the target and is considered, by some, to aid in aiming. Hunters, field archers, and

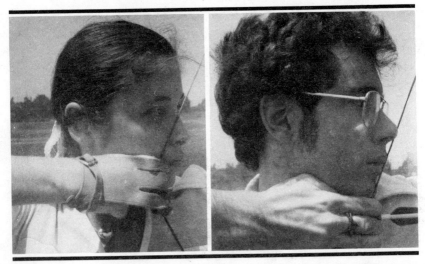

Figure 5.10 a) *High anchor position.* **b)** *Low anchor position.*

instinctive shooters usually employ a high anchor technique. The most common high anchor has the tip of the index finger at the corner of the mouth so that the top of the hand rests along the lower part of the cheekbone. Placement of the forefinger in the corner of the mouth helps to establish a definite point of contact and aids in lining up the arrow under the sighting eye.

In low anchor the forefinger rests directly under the jawbone so that the string is in line with the center of the face. The string actually touches the tip of the nose and the center of the chin. Many archers purse their lips and actually kiss the string. If the contour of the face is such that it is difficult to get the finger under the chin, if may be placed along the side of the jawbone so that its tip rests in the center of the chin. The low anchor position has advantages in sighting and allows for greater cast. The low anchor is favored by target archers and most expert freestyle shooters. Either anchor can be successfully used in any situation.

The high anchor is usually taught first. As the student gains in experience and becomes more familiar with the use and functions of the equipment, the low anchor is introduced. A common fallacy among novice archers is that a different anchor point or draw length is needed for each shooting distance. If the arrow is to fly at the same velocity each time, the draw length and anchor must be the same each time. Adjustments for distance and direction are made in the aim, not by variations in the holding position. Why use "by guess and by gosh" when it is possible to determine how much and how far? Why attempt to learn what amounts to five or six different skills when it is necessary to learn only one? Once the shooter is familiar with the relationships of trajectory, draw length, anchor point, and aim, the logic of a consistent position becomes evident.

Aiming

The use of some type of device, such as a bow sight or a point-of-aim marker, characterizes freestyle (sight) shooting. Absence of an aiming device is identified with instinctive or bare-bow shooting. Aiming enables an archer to be more accurate in his arrow placement. Different procedures are used by different archers with varying degrees of success. The advantages provided by a bow sight cannot be overstated. However, any mechanical instrument or device is of little help until the archer becomes proficient in the performance of the fundamentals and is able to group his arrows. For this reason beginning archers are usually introduced to shooting and aiming by the instinctive or bare-bow method.

Bare-Bow or Instinctive Aiming.   To shoot without a sight or point-of-aim marker, the bow is drawn to the anchor (usually a high one at first) and the eyes are focused on the exact center of the intended target. The elevation of the bow arm almost automatically adjusts itself as the archer concentrates on the intended impact area rather than on the tip of the arrow or the hand. After the first couple of arrows are released, feedback provides information to indicate how the bow arm must be moved (up, down, and/or to either side). Accurate visual shooting depends upon consistent form, good eyesight, well-developed depth perception, and kinesthetic awareness on the part of the shooter.

Point of Aim. Point of aim is probably the most commonly taught means of aiming the bow. Unfortunately, this method has limitations and other

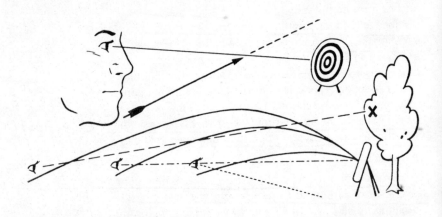

Figure 5.11 *Point of aim. Note: Arrow trajectory would be different if high anchor were used, necessitating different points of aim for the same distances.*

procedures are more appropriate. Point of aim should only serve as a temporary aiming procedure. The tip of an arrow is used like a post in a sight and aimed at some spot in front of, on, or above the target. At anchor, the tip of the arrow is usually well below the sighting eye. The aiming spot selected for a given distance depends upon the height of the shooter, length of the arrow drawn, and bow weight. It is not exactly the same for each individual. There is only one distance from the target when the tip of the arrow can be aimed directly at

its center. This distance is called *point-blank range* and
might not coincide with any of the established shooting
lines. (See Figure 5.11.) At relatively short distances, the
sighting spot is on the ground in front of the target. As
the range is increased, the spot moves closer to the
target. At extremely long distances, or with very light
bows, an aiming point above the impact area may be
needed. Point of aim for each distance is determined by
shooting several arrows and examining the groupings
which occur. Clusters below the center of the target
indicate the need to move the aiming point farther away
from the archer. High groupings or arrows over the
target necessitate moving the spot closer to the archer.

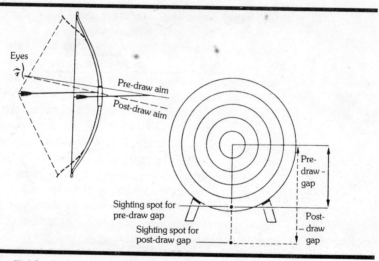

Figure 5.12 *Gap aiming. Broken lines represent gap after draw.
Solid lines represent gap before the draw.*

Gap Methods of Aiming. Pre-gap and post-gap
aim are similar to point of aim in that the archer uses the
tip of the arrow to sight to a selected spot. (See Figure
5 .12.) The distance between the desired point of entry
and the aiming spot is called the gap. In pre-gap aiming,
the bow is raised to shooting position and the tip of the
arrow aligned with a predetermined spot before the
draw. Once the bow-arm position is established, the

eyes shift to the intended target and intently focus there. The draw and subsequent release is made without altering body or head position. Post-gap aim differs from pre-gap only in that the arrow tip is placed on a spot at full draw. Both gap systems differ from point of aim in that, once the arrow is lined up, the eyes focus on the intended target, not on the aiming spot. Adjustments for errors are made by estimating the necessary change in the gap to hit the target. If the arrow falls short, the gap is lessened. The gap system merely provides a quick means for attaining some degree of proficiency with bare-bow shooting at relatively short ranges and is not regarded as the ultimate in aiming procedure.

Sight Shooting. The mechanical device attached to the back or belly of the bow provides the most accurate means of aiming. A sight is relatively easy to use and allows for more exact corrections. Once the sight position for a given distance is known, a mark is made on the device itself or on the side of the bow. Prior knowledge of sight placement means that arrows will land in approximately the right spot at the very beginning of each practice session. Relatively minor adjustments for wind and weather conditions are made after a few shots. Moving the sight up and down changes the elevation of the bow arm. As the sight moves up, the bow arm is lowered. Adjustments for right-left errors (windage) are accomplished by moving the post in or out. If the arrow goes right (for a right-handed archer), the sight is moved or pushed in toward the bow. This causes the bow arm to move so that the arrow comes more in line with the center of the target. The sight is always moved in the direction of the error. If the arrow flies high and left, the sight is moved up and out. If the arrow is low and right, the sight is moved down and in.

On occasion, difficulty in using the sight is experienced. People are generally one-sided; that is, if they are right-handed, they are also right-footed and aim with the right eye. People who are right-handed generally use the right eye for determining direction, the other eye provides distance depth perception. In some cases the dominant eye is not on the same side as the shooting hand; this can be bothersome in learning to use a sight. Check for eye dominance by pointing the index finger of the dominant hand directly at the center of a distant spot while both eyes are open. Cover the eye on the nondominant side (left eye if right-handed) and then the other eye. If the eye that is used for determining direction is on the same side as the dominant hand, the finger will continue to point at the spot when this eye is exposed, and appear to jump to the side when the eye is covered. Any movement of the finger indicates that the eye is not functioning when focusing for direction. It is possible for a person with

Figure 5.13 Release and follow-through. This graph check photograph shows how the hand will move back past the neck, toward the rear shoulder, if the draw has been executed properly using the large muscles of the back.

confused dominance to learn to shoot with a sight once he is aware of the condition.

Release

The act of sending the arrow on its path to the target could be thought of as archery's "moment of truth." All the preparation has occurred, all that remains is to loose the string. Contraction of the upper back muscles must be maintained or the hand will *creep* forward before the release, resulting in a low-flying arrow. Proper tension without strain or rigidity depends upon the archer's ability to accomplish the prerequisite phases correctly and upon his ability to free his mind of all outside distractions. The release itself is accomplished by simply relaxing the fingers. As contact with the string is broken, the action of the back muscles causes the elbow of the drawing arm to move back as the shoulder blades come together. The arm and shoulder move back as a single unit so that the hand passes alongside the neck. (See Figure 5.13.)

There is a tendency to grip the bow as the string fingers relax. Every effort should be made to see that this does not occur. Attempt to keep the bow at draw level, but avoid excessive tension. Allow the bow to move naturally; it will move very slightly down and to the side. Attention to the release is important since it is easy to introduce many errors at this particular moment. Most indoor archery ranges and some schools have specially constructed training bows. The training bow is made so that it can be safely drawn and released without an arrow. Practice with these devices helps develop kinesthetic awareness in executing a good, relaxed release. If a training bow is not available, the release can be practiced by pointing the arrow toward a nearby spot on the ground, drawing back 5″ or 6″ and relaxing the hand. A good release has the hand move backward as the string moves forward.

Follow-Through or Afterhold

If errors in parts of the form remain undetected, their existence may actually be encouraged by rehearsal during practice sessions. The follow-through involves maintaining the body, arm, and head position assumed at release until the arrow lands. What the archer does after the arrow leaves the bow does not affect the flight of the projectile. However, extension of the release posture helps to point up the mistakes in execution which occurred *before* the release. Position of the bow arm, hands, head, shoulders, etc., provides information to the performer about errors in other parts of his form. Characteristics of a proper afterhold include the following:

1. Body erect, shoulders down and back, not collapsed.

2. Head toward the target, eyes focused on the objective.

3. Bow arm in extended position, little evidence of movement.

4. Fingers holding the bow are relaxed; no appreciable grasping has occurred.

5. String hand passed back along the side of the neck, fingers relaxed, free of tension.

Figure 5.14 *Retrieving and scoring.*

Retrieving

Once the arrows are shot (hopefully into the intended target) all that remains is to collect them. Arrows impaled in a target butt are withdrawn by placing one hand on the face of the target close to the point of entry. The other hand grasps the shaft, not the fletching, near the point. The arrow is withdrawn by twisting the shaft and pulling out at the angle of entry. (See Figure 5.14.) Soft spots in some targets allow arrows to penetrate so that the fletching is fully or partly incorporated into the packing. Embedded arrows are retrieved with minor damage to the feathers by pulling them completely through the back side of the target. Ground arrows are collected in much the same manner as those hitting a target. If the fletching is free of entanglement, the arrow is removed nock first. To retrieve buried arrows, the point is located and the arrow pulled forward through the clutter until it is free. Special care should be exercised when securing glass- and aluminum-shafted arrows. Glass shafts can be broken when stepped on and aluminum shafts are bent if pressure is incorrectly applied during removal.

ANALYSIS OF PERFORMANCE

The objective of the shooting act is to have the arrows reach the intended target. Certain errors seem to occur regularly when shooting is first started. Generally speaking, these can be classified according to the hit (or miss) on the target. More than one factor can affect accuracy, and one error may cancel the effect of another. Observation by another person (instructor or student coach) is helpful in analyzing archery form. Faults are often very subtle or occur quickly, so the observer must be aware of what to look for. Tables 1 and 2 indicate some of the more common shooting problems and provide information for correcting the difficulty.

TABLE 1

Analysis of the Fundamentals

DIFFICULTY	PROBABLE CAUSE	SUGGESTED CORRECTION
Incorrect head position — tilted or forward.	1. Face not turned directly toward target.	1. Assume stance, looking straight ahead, then turn face toward target, keep head in this position throughout execution.
Arrow falls away from bow.	1. Fingers used to draw the string instead of merely acting as hooks.	1. Have elbow back at beginning; use back muscles to draw; practice partial draw, checking finger and hand position. Hand flattens as soon as elbow begins to move back if used properly.
	2. Pinching nock of arrow between index and middle finger.	2. Finger should contact arrow nock lightly, no pressure. Place emphasis on drawing the string back, not the arrow. Try letting the fingers roll or twist the string during the draw; helps keep the arrow in the bow.
Too much extension or straightness of bow arm.	1. Arrow too long. 2. Excessive pressure in pushing bow out.	1. Use shorter arrow, but be careful to avoid an overdraw. 2. Place emphasis on draw, not on pushing bow away.
Grasping or squeezing bow.	1. Using muscles of bow hand to grip.	1. Work for relaxed wrist and hand. Have only index finger and thumb around grip, exert very slight pressure. Practice string release with bow hand, work for relaxed wrist and hand as string leaves fingers. Use a finger sling.
Failure to hold anchor long enough.	1. Bow too heavy. 2. Tendency to "snap shoot," or shoot too rapidly.	1. Use a lighter bow until sufficient strength is developed. 2. Draw and hold anchor position for several seconds before releasing. Practice draw, hold, while aiming at a mirror or some object that has value to you. (Not a person, if you please.)

TABLE 1 (Continued)

DIFFICULTY	PROBABLE CAUSE	SUGGESTED CORRECTION
Hunched bow shoulder.	1. Bow too strong.	1. Use lightest bow possible. Check arrow length; a shorter one may be needed. Practice fundamentals. Concentrate on keeping forward shoulder down and back. Experiment with open stance, which forces shoulder down when aiming.
Aiming with eye on the bow-arm side	1. Inability to close the nonsighting eye. 2. Sighting with the eye on the non-dominant side.	1. Practice winking the eye to strengthen muscles of the eyelid. 2. Check for dominant eye. Keep non-dominant eye closed when aiming.
Hitting elbow of bow arm at release.	1. Arm hyperextended. 2. Attempting to draw an arrow that is too long.	1. Rotate elbow down and out in such a way that, if flexion were to occur, the bow would swing into body (chest). Practice correct position mimetically or with a training bow until position becomes easy to assume. 2. Check for correct arrow length and use those closest to the exact measurement.
Bow string repeatedly hits wrist.	1. Brace height incorrect.	1. Check correct bracing height; shorten string by twisting.
Bruise or cuts on top part of bow hand or upper finger.	1. Finger or hand held so that arrow touches it when leaving bow. 2. Rough feathers; glue deposits usually at base of cock feather.	1. Check hand position; use bow with an arrow rest, if possible. 2. Sand area and wax.

TABLE 2

Analysis of Directional Errors

ARROW PLACEMENT	PROBABLE CAUSE	SUGGESTED CORRECTIONS
Arrows scattered; no consistent pattern or grouping.	1. Faulty arrows — shaft bent or warped, vanes uneven or damaged. 2. Arrows not matched properly. 3. Inconsistent form. 4. Inability to hold a stable position. 5. Arrow releases before proper aim has been accomplished.	1. Check arrows; replace those damaged or bent. 2. Use matched set, if possible. 3. Review and practice fundamentals. 4. Use a lighter bow; exercise to increase muscular strength. 5. Practice draw and hold.
Arrows fly high or over the target (12 o-clock).	*General* 1. Sight too low; point of aim too close to target; gap too small. 2. "Peeking" or looking up at release. 3. Body "recoils" (moves back) at release. 4. Heavier bow or different arrows than those normally used. *Grip and Bow Arm* 1. Bow arm moves up or straightens at release. 2. Forefinger lifted, causing arrow to be raised above plate or rest. *String arm and hand* 1. Arrow nocked too low. 2. String pulled with less than three fingers; third finger allowed to slip off first. 3. Lower jaw dropped (mouth opened); anchor lower than normal. 4. "Jerking" (backward movement of hand *before* release). 5. Bow overdrawn.	1. Move sight up; move aiming point closer to shooting line; increase size of gap. 2. Concentrate on target; hold head steady until arrow hits. 3. Hold body position steady until arrow hits. 4. Use same equipment each day of shooting or allow for adjustment when changing tackle. 1. Work on holding proper bow-arm position. 2. Check grip; correct finger position. 1. Make adjustment and mark proper nocking point. 2. Place three fingers on string properly; work for complete relaxation of hand at release; practice partial draw and release into ground. 3. Keep mouth in original position; use consistent anchor. 4. Hold anchor position, work for relaxed finger release. 5. Use same anchor for each shot; check bow-arm and shoulder position.

TABLE 2 (Continued)

ARROW PLACEMENT	PROBABLE CAUSE	SUGGESTED CORRECTIONS
Arrows fly low or fall short of the target (6 o'clock).	*General* 1. Sight too low; spot too close to archer; gap too large. 2. Arrow released before full draw or before sight is properly aligned. 3. Leaning or moving upper body forward at release. 4. Bow understrung. 5. Insufficient bow power. 6. Failure to compensate for a "headwind."	1. Adjust sight (move down); select spot closer to target; shorten gap. 2. Come to full draw and hold until properly "sighted in." Use a draw check device on the bow. 3. Maintain erect posture. 4. Check and correct brace height. 5. Use heavier bow or move to a low anchor. 6. Make sight adjustments to allow for wind conditions.
	Grip and bow arm 1. Bow arm drops or collapses at release. 2. Bow arm fatigued, tends to "give." 3. Grip too low on bow.	1. Hold follow-through; try to maintain elevation of bow arm without increasing tension. 2. Do not hold anchor and aim position so long that muscles tire; work to strengthen drawing muscles. 3. Put bow hand nearer top edge of grip.
	String arm and hand 1. "Creeping" (arrow moves forward before release). 2. Draw elbow lowered on release. 3. Arrow nocked too high.	1. Keep anchor firm; work to strengthen drawing muscles. 2. Make sure elbow moves directly back; keep it slightly above the shoulder when drawing. 3. Put a nocking point on the string ⅛" to ¼" above the 90° angle formed by the arrow and the string; nock the arrow below this point.
Arrows go left (9 o'clock for right-handed shooter).	*General* 1. Right-handed shooter (with dominant right eye) using left eye for aiming. (Arrows travel extremely left.)	1. Close or cover left eye; practice using right eye to aim.

TABLE 2 (Continued)

ARROW PLACEMENT	PROBABLE CAUSE	SUGGESTED CORRECTIONS
	2. Bow string not sighted correctly.	2. Head should be held so that the line of vision is slightly to the right of the string and to the left of bow or directly through the string; the string is lined up with the left side of the sight window so that there is no space visible; check string alignment on bow.
	3. Arrows too stiffly spined for bow (arrows slightly left).	3. Match bow and arrows; use heavier bow with same arrows; change arrows to more flexible ones for use with same bow.
	4. Failure to compensate for wind blowing to the left.	4. Make windage adjustments for conditions (sight moves out, or to left, for right-handed shooter).
	Grip and bow arm	
	1. Bow canted, upper limb tilted to the left.	1. Have bow perpendicular; check with horizon; check pressure of bow grip; check head position; face directly toward target.
	2. Bow gripped too tightly, especially fingers on right side of bow.	2. Place only thumb and forefinger around bow; put pressure into the belly of the bow; have bow contact heel of hand throughout.
	3. Flinching of the bow arm.	3. Wear arm guard for protection and to prevent injury.
	4. Bow arm thrown to left at release.	4. Hold follow-through; work for relaxed bow arm; bow will move *very* slightly to side and down naturally.
	5. Wrist hyperextended; string to right of left edge of bow at full draw.	5. Move wrist in line directly behind hand; check sight line through string and left side of bow.
	6. String hits arm or clothing.	6. Wear appropriate clothing; remove jewelry or objects on left side of body; have shoulder go *down* and *back* in the draw.
	String arm and hand	
	1. Not enough fingers on string; string held too close to tips.	1. Three fingers should be used as hooks on the string; move string closer to first joint or use "deep" hook.
	2. "Plucking" — hand moves away from face sideways at release.	2. Hand and arm should move back along the side of the neck. Practice release; keep string in firm contact until release.
	3. Arrow squeezed.	3. Avoid putting pressure on arrow nock; string fingers only hooks; use back and upper arm muscles for draw.
	4. Anchor away from the side of the face.	4. Use a solid anchor with consistent points of contact on the face; practice mimetics of shooting.

TABLE 2 (Continued)

ARROW PLACEMENT	PROBABLE CAUSE	SUGGESTED CORRECTIONS
Arrows travel right for right-handed archer (3-o'clock).	*General* 1. Stance closed, left foot not in line with or drawn back from right foot.	1. Check foot position; be sure string is correctly aligned with side of bow at full draw.
	2. Arrows too flexible, weakly spined (goes slightly right).	2. Match bow and arrows; use stiffer arrow with same bow; use same arrows with lighter bow.
	3. Aiming with left eye (which is dominant) when shooting right-handed.	3. Learn to shoot left-handed if it is discovered early that left eye is dominant eye; point of aim or place where sight is held must be aligned left of intended target if right-handed shooting continues.
	4. Upper limb canted or tilted right.	4. Bow should be perpendicular; check grip; put pressure into belly of the bow; check head position for tilting.
	5. No allowance for wind blowing to right.	5. Move stance and adjust aim to compensate for wind conditions (sight moves right, closer to bow), may be necessary to select an object to left of target to aim at if wind deflection is severe.
	6. Feathers on arrow too large.	6. Feathers should be trimmed to size to match weight of arrow shaft.
	Grip and bow arm 1. Bow hand and arm thrown to right at release.	1. Work for controlled relaxation of left wrist at release; check left wrist for flexion; use back muscles for draw; check bow shoulder position (a hunched shoulder can contribute to the arm moving forward and to the right).
	2. Bow arm collapses to right across body on release.	2. Maintain elevation of bow arm.
	3. Gripping wrist flexed.	3. Move wrist to position directly behind hand.
	String hand and arm 1. String to left of left side of bow at full draw.	1. Check line of vision through string and edge of bow; no space or gap showing.
	2. String jerked to left on or just before release.	2. Hold anchor firm until release; work for relaxed finger release so hand and arm move straight back.

BASIC SAFETY CONSIDERATIONS

Archery is not dangerous; people are! The bow and arrow is a weapon and should be considered as such. Weapons possess the potential to seriously injure or permanently maim if used without discretion.

General Safety

1. Develop safety consciousness.
2. Shoot only in appropriate areas.
3. Allow sufficient space between archers.
4. Nock arrows only when the shooting area is clear.
5. Don't draw the bow back with an arrow unless you are going to shoot.
6. Always have a definite target at which to aim. Shooting arrows straight into the air is dangerous and rather senseless.
7. Avoid wearing clothes or jewelry that may catch the bow string.
8. Practice courtesy and consideration of others.

Safety in the Technique of Shooting

1. Avoid a stiff, straight bow arm. The arm should be rotated out. When the arm is in correct position, the bow will move directly toward the body when the elbow is flexed.
2. The index finger of the bow hand should be around the handle, not alongside the arrow, on release.
3. Always use an arm guard and finger protection.
4. Keep the bow arm in proper position to avoid an overdraw.
5. Never point an arrow at anyone, whether the bow is drawn or not.
6. Step back from the shooting line until everyone has finished shooting.

Safety on the Range and at the Target

1. Use a common shooting line. Move the targets to allow archers to practice at different distances at the same time.

2. Check to see that the targets are firmly anchored.

3. Check for rocks in the shooting area.

4. Stand away from the person withdrawing arrows from the target.

5. When shooting in a group, retrieving and shooting should not be carried on at the same time. Even when targets are far apart there is danger of an arrow glancing to the right or left and hitting someone who is retrieving.

Safety with the Bow

1. Never release the string without an arrow.

2. Check the bow string regularly for frayed string or serving.

3. Bows which have been stored for some time or that have been in the cold should be warmed up gradually.

4. Check the bow for cracks or splintering.

5. Check the brace height of the bow regularly.

6. Do not use a bow that is too heavy for you.

7. When bracing the bow, follow several precautions: (a) make sure the lower end is properly secured at the foot; (b) apply pressure equally at three points; (c) be careful not to get the fingers caught under the string; (d) be sure both ends of the string are entirely in the notches.

8. Do not overdraw, as the bow may break.

Safety with Arrows

1. Avoid using cracked or split arrows; check arrows after each end.

2. Take care in drawing accurately; the arrow may go wild or into the hand if overdrawn.

3. Be sure the arrow is of sufficient length.

4. If the arrow slips when drawing, start over; don't push up with the finger and keep drawing or the arrow may be released too soon and fly wild.

5. Avoid pinching the nock at release.

SUGGESTED TASKS FOR THE LEARNER

(NOTE: These tasks should be performed in a safe manner. It would be wise to secure the instructor's permission before attempting them.)

1. Practice putting on the arm guard and finger tab or glove. Check with the instructor to see if you are doing it properly.

2. Brace the bow several times, using the procedures described. "Talk" someone else through the stringing process.

3. Shoot arrows nocked in the manner indicated in the text and also with the index feather turned toward the bow. Check for differences in flight and for damage to the fletching.

4. Experiment with the shallow hook and the deep hook. Determine which technique is most comfortable and results in the smoothest release.

5. Draw a diagram of the flight of your arrows to a target from a distance of 40 yards using a high anchor position. Draw a diagram of the arrow's trajectory using a low anchor for the same distance. What conclusion can you draw from your pictures?

6. Construct a homemade bow sight.

6

BEYOND THE FUNDAMENTALS

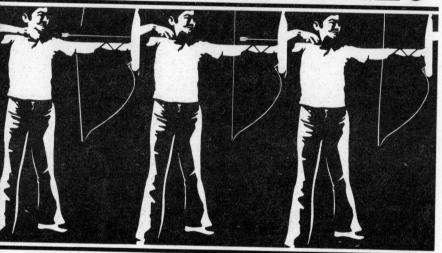

Once the archer has had some success in executing the fundamentals, there is usually a desire not only to improve performance, but also to learn more about the technical and psychological aspects of the sport. While it is possible to develop a high degree of competence with relatively simple and inexpensive materials, use of more sophisticated equipment can aid in reaching your real potential. In addition to proper selection, the archer must also know how to *set up* and *tune* the bow if he is to maximize the advances made by our modern bowyers. Mental as well as physical preparation is necessary in order to perform well under the pressures of tournament conditions. This chapter presents additional information on equipment, provides instruction on proper set up and tuning of the bow, gives suggestions for refinement of technique, and considers some psychological points related to shooting.

EQUIPMENT

Determination of suitable tackle involves some experimentation. Time spent in the process will prove worthwhile if the result is acquisition of tools suited to individual physical characteristics and shooting style. Having confidence in your equipment tends to build confidence in your ability to perform, and this pays dividends when scores are tallied at the end of each round.

Bows

Bows differ in length, weight, limb design, and handle configuration. Individual draw length is a factor in selecting an appropriate bow. As a rule of thumb, if the draw is 28″, a 68″ bow is recommended; for a 25″ draw, 66″ would be appropriate. Weight-in-hand is another factor; the more serious tournament archer tends to prefer a slightly heavier bow, as this is considered an asset in steadying the arm. Draw weight will vary, depending on individual strength, but should be as heavy as the person can handle and still shoot in a relaxed, comfortable manner. Choice of configuration of the handle or riser is another personal matter; experimentation with several variations will soon show which type is most helpful in promoting a consistent grip.

The most recent innovation in the art of bow-making is the compound bow (see Figure 6.1). This revolutionary design incorporates a system of pulleys and cables that produce mechanical advantage. Drawing this type of bow is an interesting experience, as you can actually feel a reduction in the effort needed to pull the string as the bow approaches full draw position. The greater velocity (over 200 ft/sec) possible with the compound bow is one of the features which makes it attractive to hunters. The flatter trajectory associated with increased arrow speed has obvious advantages for

the target archer as well. However, because of its unique
string arrangement, the bow does not meet NAA or FITA
standards for all forms of competition, which limits its
use for target events to some extent.

Composite working recurve bows are almost the
exclusive choice of today's target enthusiasts. While
most bows of this type appear to be very similar, it is
wise to try several different models, as shooting
characteristics vary widely. Smoothness in draw and
release with no "stacking up" as the bow is drawn to
anchor is one factor to consider. Many recurves are
designed so that they can be collapsed or taken apart
when not in use. While this type of bow has been
around for some time, recent technical improvements
have caused it to gain popularity among serious
competitors. Ease of storage and transport are among
the characteristics which make this bow desirable.
Another point is that limbs of different draw weights can
be purchased to fit the same riser, enabling the bow to
be used in a variety of situations. The interchangeable-
limb feature allows the archer to move to progressively
heavier draw weights as strength is increased or, since
there is nothing in the rules to prohibit it, to use heavier
limbs for longer distances and lighter ones at shorter
distances. This might be helpful in warding off fatigue in
the later rounds of competition.

Stabilizers

Introduction of the stabilizer has led to a marked
improvement in scores. Since there are several styles
and shapes available, it is necessary to determine which
type or types, in combination with the rest of the tackle,
produces the best groupings. The most common design
is a rod with a metal weight at the end which is attached
to the lower part of the riser. Some stabilizers are made
so that weight can be varied. There are also types which
have adjustments to stiffen or soften the coupler which
attaches the shaft to the bow (see Figure 6.2). The
added weight and actual forward shift in the center of
gravity of the bow help to steady the arm when sighting.
The extentions also aid in absorbing release shock and
in preventing bow torque (horizontal twisting or left-right
bow movement). This greater stability and lack of

torquing minimize the effect of technique errors, and the result is better scores. Current rules permit the use of up to four stabilizers, provided they do not touch anything but the bow and are positioned so that they do not interfere with other shooters on the line (see Figure 6.3).

Sighting Aids

A good mechanical sight with finite settings for vertical and horizontal adjustment is essential tackle for the competitive archer. There are a number of other aids which are useful in attaining proficiency with the sight, including sight extenders, kisser buttons, peep or string sights, and bow levels.

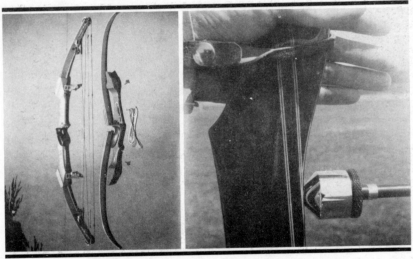

Figure 6.1 *Left—compound bow. Right—left-handed take-down bow.*
Figure 6.2 *Adjustable coupler for stabilizer. Note bow sling on archer's hand.*

Sight Extenders. This mechanism, attached to either the side or the back of the bow, allows the sight to be placed farther out in front of the archer (see Figure 6.4). Theoretically, the increased distance between the aiming eye and the aperture helps in minimizing error by forcing the archer to aim more accurately. As the distance between the bow and the sight is increased, the field of vision through the opening is decreased and thus the archer must focus on a more precise point. The extender also permits the sight to be placed closer to the bow or even reversed. This is advantageous at longer distances as it allows archers with weaker bows to still sight on the target.

Kisser Button. Another aid in attaining consistency in draw position is the kisser button. This device, usually made of plastic, is attached to the bow string above the nocking point and is positioned in such a way that, at full draw with a low anchor position, the disc will rest between the lips. Kisser buttons are one of the few legal shooting aids in both NAA and FITA competitions.

Figure 6.3 *Bow equipped with two stabilizers. Weight can be adjusted by adding or subtracting metal at the end.*
Figure 6.4 *Sight extender. Another advantage of the sight extender is that is allows the sight to be moved closer or even reversed for shooting at longer distances.*

String Peep. Peep sights are plastic or metal accessories that come in two shapes—round or elongated. When properly inserted into the string above the serving, the aiming eye will sight through the hole·or slot and line up the pin in the bow sight with the target. Practice with this device is helpful in promoting proper head alignment and a consistent anchor point. However, the archer is cautioned not to become too dependent on its use, as FITA rounds cannot be shot using this aid.

Levels. A bubble mechanism, similar to a carpenter's level, attached to the sight or to the bow itself provides visual feedback as to horizontal bow position. Use of a level helps in attaining consistent alignment and thus helps develop accuracy. Again, discrimination in use is recommended, as the device is not legal in sanctioned events.

Bow or Finger Slings. The use of a bow sling or finger sling promotes a loose, relaxed bow hand, which

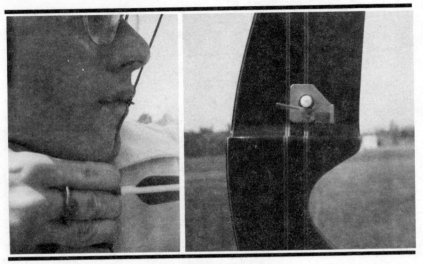

Figure 6.5 *Archer using the Kisser button.*
Figure 6.6 *Cushion plunger and swing-away arrow rest.*

is characteristic of good archery technique. The sling keeps the bow under control during release and follow-through and lessens the tendency to tighten the grip as the arrow is loosed; this allows the archer to concentrate on the release without worrying about dropping the bow. The bow sling encircles or attaches to the bow and slips over the wrist, allowing the bow to be cradled by the hand. The finger sling consists of a short piece of material with loops at either end. The thumb and index finger are inserted in the openings, with the solid part of the material across the back of the bow. Homemade finger slings can be manufactured with scrap pieces of leather slitted at both ends, or by forming loops in a short length of nylon cord.

Adjustable Arrow Plates

Adjustable arrow plates are almost essential for the fine tuning of the bow. While it is possible to tune a bow by adding or subtracting material from the portion of the sight window against which the arrow rests, it is far more convenient to install an adjustable arrow plate or cushion plunger (see Figure 6.6). The cushion plunger is

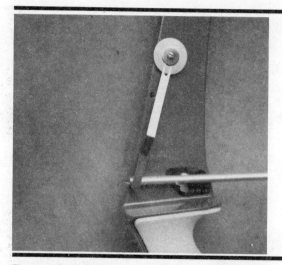

Figure 6.7 Clicker mechanism. The clicker can be used simply as a draw check or as a release signal.

mounted into the sight window just above the arrow rest. The amount of protrusion, as well as the degree of tension on the spring, can be regulated. When precisely set for the tackle used, the loaded action of the cushion plunger absorbs forces that bend the arrow and thus helps arrows leave the bow in a straighter line.

Clicker

Precision in the length of the draw is a must if tight groupings are to be attained. A clicker mechanism consists of a piece of metal attached to a pressure-sensitive backing which is affixed on the sight window (see Figure 6.7). The device is positioned so that the metal strip extends over the shaft of the arrow. When the arrow has been drawn the proper length, the clicker snaps back onto the bow, making a noise that signals full draw position. Some archers use the audible click as a signal for release; others use it simply as a draw check.

Arrows

Although more expensive, aluminum arrows are preferred by serious competitors, and the purchase of a good set of this type of arrow should be considered

Figure 6.8 A properly fitting nock will cling to the string, as shown here.

before buying other desirable, but less essential, tackle. Care should be taken to ensure that the arrows are compatible with the bow in use; a good archery shop will provide help in this respect. Most of today's top tournament shooters have opted for plastic fletchings, as plastic vanes are lighter and more uniform in weight and will not be affected by rain or humidity. This type of fletch is less ''forgiving'' than feathers, however, and tends to magnify errors due to faulty technique. This factor should be carefully weighed in making a purchase decision.

The nock end of the arrow is another important consideration in precision shooting. The nock should fit the string with just enough tightness to allow it to cling without falling off (see Figure 6.8). The Bjorn Nock has this characteristic built in; it is possible, however, to apply heat to the more common type of nock and squeeze it to create the desired pinching effect.

SET UP AND TUNING

Many experienced archers are not aware of how to get maximum performance from their tackle. As has been mentioned previously, arrows must be matched to the bow by determining actual draw weight (see Chapter 4). If the arrows are of proper spine and weight, there are a number of other procedures which need to be regularly attended to if perfect arrow flight is the goal.

Brace Height

Each manufacturer indicates the appropriate brace height for each model of bow. Do not assume all recurves have the same specifications; as heights vary considerably, depending on the design of the bow. Once the brace height is known, care should be taken to ensure that the distance is consistent from one outing to the next.

After warming up the strung bow by pullng back and letting down several times, measure the distance from the string to the pivot point, or saddle, in the handle. If the distance is less than that recommended, remove the string from the upper limb, make six or more turns, and then check again. If more than twelve turns are needed to shorten the string, it should be replaced.

It is permissible to increase or decrease the recommended brace height to suit individual preference. A greater distance, provided it is not overdone, will add cast to the bow, which is desirable for some archers. A decrease in distance results in less string vibration and a smoother bow. However, if the brace height is too narrow, the result will be painful wrist slaps as well as loss of cast. Remember that changing the distance of the string from the bow affects the position of the nocking point.

Brace height should be checked periodically during competitive and practice rounds, as strings do stretch and this will cause a variation from the desired nocking point. Fine tuning should also be done regularly, and especially before competitive events. Straightness of arrows and proper nock alignment are other factors which need to be checked if the tackle is to perform for the competitor.

Set Up

Before the bow can be tuned, it is necessary to locate a temporary nocking point. With the bow properly warmed and the brace height checked, a bow square or straight edge is used to find the point on the string that is at a right angle (90°) to the arrow rest. Mark the spot and place an arrow in position over it; make another mark ⅛" above the arrow nock. This establishes a temporary nocking point. A permanent nocking point is located by fine-tuning the bow.

Arrows which wobble from side to side or up and down on their flight to the target are indicative of a poorly set up or improperly tuned bow. If up-and-down movement is the problem, the nocking point needs to be adjusted. Stand six feet away from the target and, with the bare arrow (one without fletchings), shoot the arrow at eye level into the target. If the nock end is below horizontal, the nocking point should be raised; if it is above this plane, the point should be lowered. Continue to shoot until the pattern of each arrow shot is the same. Place a nocking clip—or a knot made of dental floss secured with contact glue—at the spot established; this is the permanent nocking point. (See Figure 6.9.) A word of caution: when performing the test, take care not to vary the pressure of the fingers of your draw hand. This also applies during regular shooting.

Tuning

A phenomenon known as the *archer's paradox* is one of the reasons it is necessary to have correctly spined arrows for a given draw weight. The action of the string and bow at release produces a stress effect on the arrow, causing it to bend around the bow. As the arrow is cast, the nock end deviates first left, then right, then left again causing temporary bends in the shaft; eventually the arrow stabilizes itself in flight. While this flexing cannot be detected with the naked eye, high-speed photography has documented the action. Spine which is too strong can cause the fletching to strike the bow and deflect the arrow. Too weak a spine may not allow the arrow to stabilize during flight. If the arrows are of proper spine and fishtailing or wobbling is still evident, adjustments on the arrow plate of the bow should remedy the situation. Often wavering cannot be visually detected, so it is wise to tune the bow regularly to ensure a good flight pattern.

Again, stand six feet away and cast bare arrows at eye level into the target. If the nock is to the left of the intended line of flight, the arrow plate needs to be built out more from the bow. Nocks bearing right indicate a need to move the arrow closer to the sight window; this could involve sanding the bow itself. Make any adjustments necessary until the arrows enter the target in a straight position. Adjustable arrow plates or cushion type of plungers are beneficial for ease of tuning and are recommended if cost is not a consideration.

REFINING TECHNIQUE

Refinement of technique involves standardizing movements and analyzing errors in order to correct problems. It should be kept in mind that, as experience increases, experimentation with variations on the fundamentals discussed in Chapter 5 can be helpful in establishing the most effective form for a given individual. To determine the style best suited to you, practice the basics until you obtain some degree of consistency, and then experiment to develop the technique most comfortable for you. Consideration should be given to some of the points which follow.

Stance

Try shooting with both the square and slightly open stance as well as with a more pronounced oblique position. Along with variations in foot and hip alignment, alter the width and weight distribution. Once the most effective position has been determined, use it consistently.

Bow Hold

A slightly lower flexed wrist position might be more conducive to top performance than those discussed earlier. An effort should be made to see that the bow rests comfortably in position; pushing forward with the palm helps to relax the hand and fingers. Handles can be shaped by scraping and sanding to a contour that permits the pressure point to be more readily felt; this may prove helpful in establishing a good hold. If the bow is held too low, with the pressure in the heel of the hand, string slaps will occur. Pressure with the fingers on the sides may result in the nock hitting the sight window as the arrow is loosed.

Figure 6.9 *Arrow properly positioned below the nocking point. Note the location of the Kisser Button on serving.*

String Alignment

Alignment of the string with the bow was discussed earlier, but the novice usually has too many problems in the initial learning stages to focus on this. Once the archer has experience with the sight shooting, attention should be given to proper string alignment. Sight windows have different depths and it is not sufficient merely to line up the string with the side of the opening. Ideally, at full draw the string should be centered on the upper limb of the bow, although some variation is permissible. The range for acceptable string alignment is from the center of the bow to the sighting device; Figures 6.10 and 6.11 show acceptable and unacceptable positions. Again, once the line is established, it should be used consistently.

String Pressure

While some instructors emphasize equal pressure on each of the string fingers and others stress more pressure on the middle finger, this is not necessarily best for all shooters. Experiment with variations in pressure, but remember that whatever pressure is preferred, it should be used regularly. Be sure to tune the bow for each

Figure 6.10 *Acceptable string-alignment position.*
Figure 6.11 *Unacceptable string-alignment position — the string is much too far to the right.*

experimental session, as changes in finger pressure affect the dynamics of the bow.

Draw

A technique which employs what is known as a primary and secondary draw is advocated by some instructors and coaches. In this method, the draw is thought of as having two stages. In the first stage the bow is pulled back to anchor position and the archer concentrates on aiming. The second phase involves a conscious tightening of the back and shoulder muscles, which triggers the release. Thinking of the draw in this manner and practicing it, both mentally and physically, should help the archer develop a better feel and should result in a smooth, consistent release.

Aiming

There are two theories concerning the focus point for sight shooting. One theory contends that the archer should see the center of the gold clearly and view the string and sight aperture as blurs. The other theory advocates a clear picture of the string alignment and sight, with the target a distant blur. Obviously, it is not possible to see two objects a considerable distance apart clearly at the same time, so each person must decide which theory works best for him and use one to the exclusion of the other. Supporters of the close-vision technique (sight and string clear, target blurred) maintain that this method allows for better control of windage.

Rhythm

Success in archery depends on being able to do the exact same thing, in the exact same manner, each and every time. Obviously, man is not a machine and cannot be expected to replicate a given task as precisely as a finely tooled mechanism. However, the closer he can come to reproducing the same action with each shot, the more consistent his scoring will be. Each individual should work toward developing a distinct pattern for the shooting act. Once this is established, even minor deviations in technique can be detected through kinesthetic sense (feel) and thus prevent a wasted shot. Some shooters find it helpful to use a mental checklist. While specific cues will vary from person to person, the following should be considered in making a selection: relax; concentrate/visualize; nock; extend; draw; anchor; tighten/hold; aim; tighten/release; follow through.

PSYCHOLOGICAL CONSIDERATIONS

Conditioning + confidence + concentration = consistency, and consistency is the key to success. A successful archer is not necessarily the person who wins the tournament, takes the target prize, or shoots a championship-level score. The successful archer is the one who sets realistic goals for himself, commits himself to those goals, and does everything necessary to achieve them. This is as true for the recreational participant as it is for the professional; the difference is in the nature of the goals that are sought, not in the process.

Earlier it was mentioned that archery is one of the few sports in which it is possible to achieve championship-level performance in a relatively short period of time. While this level of aspiration might be realistic for some, it is not appropriate for all. Establishing personal goals requires some self-assessment. Ask yourself your reasons for participation—competition, sociability, relaxation, diversion, challenge? What are your qualifications for the level of competition in which you wish to participate? What do you need to do to improve your skill and strength? How do you feel about your ability to learn? How much do you really want to improve, and how much are you willing to pay for it in terms of time and effort? How much time do you have to devote to practice and competition? Answers to these and other questions provide a basis for setting realistic expectations and formulating a plan to reach your objectives.

Enjoyment of the experience is as important to success as shooting an ideal score. Keep in mind that it is possible to become a champion in the full enjoyment of sport no matter what your level of ability; just make sure the challenge you set is of your own design—one which meets *your* needs and gives *you* satisfaction. In this way you can be assured of attaining all the benefits—psychological, physical, and social—that can accrue from participation.

Practice

Practice sessions are important for conditioning, perfecting skill, building confidence, and developing the ability to concentrate. Unfortunately, many people do not realize that there are different forms of practice. In addition, most people do not know how to make the most effective use of the time they have available to them. The purpose of practice sessions is to bring the mind and body to a state that allows the best chance for peak performance. Use of mental rehearsal and sensory practice to supplement regular physical practice is helpful in this regard.

Mental Rehearsal. Psychologists often refer to mental practice as *imagery* because instructions are presented to the body in picture form, as images. The technique has been sucessfully employed by athletes in a wide variety of sports. Basically, the procedure involves mentally rehearsing the *correct* physical action of the skill. In doing imagery, the skill is broken down into its parts and mentally rehearsed sequentially, sometimes in slow motion, sometimes at normal speed. It is important that the action be pictured from start to successful conclusion. The more vivid and detailed the image, the better, as this helps make the desired pattern more automatic. Mental rehearsal aids in building confidence and concentration because it forces the learner to focus on the action and block out extraneous distractions. Imagery does not involve the use of equipment or space; it can be done any place and any time you are free of other responsibilities. Practice time is at a premium for most of us, and mental rehearsal is a way of making more practice time available.

Sensory Practice. Development of muscle memory is an important part of learning a motor skill. Golfers and baseball players often take swings to get a sense of feel before actual execution, and this helps reinforce correct motions. Archers shoot practice rounds and take practice ends before competition for the same reason. But in these situations the emphasis is placed on the visual aspects, not on the physical sensation. Research has demonstrated that when vision is blocked out, inner physical sensations become more pronounced. The experience helps reinforce memory and allows the act to be more readily duplicated under pressure.

Essentially, sensory practice is going through the motions of the activity with your eyes closed in order to heighten your awareness of your body during the act. First the movement is practiced as deliberately and correctly as possible with the eyes open; then it is repeated with the eyes closed. As this is done, attention should be given to how your body feels, where the balance is, and when and where the power from your muscles is applied. You should open your eyes at various points to see that the details of position are correct. Any deviation from desired form should be thought through in an effort to seek the cause and correct it. Needless to say, for safety's sake, a partner should be involved and the shooting distance limited.

Shooting Practice. Actual shooting sessions are the primary means of developing the confidence and concentration necessary to perform up to expectation under pressure conditions. In general, unless you are working on some particular phase of shooting technique or experimenting with style variations, your practice sessions should simulate actual tournament conditions. Scores for the rounds should be recorded and logged for informational purposes. Practicing in this manner is beneficial on two counts. First, it gives experience in shooting rounds that are included in the tournament schedule—those currently used in competition. Second, because you record all scores, comparisons can be made between tournament and practice scores. Knowing your average score for given rounds and distances is an aid in measuring progress, establishing realistic goals for improvement, and setting up expectations for competitive events. Practice sessions which simulate tournament setting will provide you with a feel for the actual situation. Practice will also help in developing an appropriate pace so that fatigue does not become a negative factor, and it has psychological benefits as well.

Most athletes concur that the ability to concentrate makes the difference between a good performance and a mediocre one. Concentration is an intangible; you must have it to make the shots—without it the arrow will not do what you want it to do. Pressure can cause anxiety, doubt, frustration, and discouragement. Once these enter your mind you get angry and start to lose what little concentration you had. Concentration is focusing attention on what is taking place at the moment and excluding anything not pertinent to the subject. It is the process of conditioning the mind to do what you need it to do. Your mind has the same need for conditioning as your body, and this conditioning is achieved in the same way—through work and self-discipline. Development of a systematic shooting style which includes a pause between shots to relax and refocus your thoughts is part of the process. Practice sessions which simulate competition, supplemented by sensory and mental rehearsal, also contribute to development of concentration.

Programming for Success

If you are to realize the real rewards of participation, you must determine what it is you wish to get from the experience. You need to know your personal reasons for engaging in archery—or any other sport, for that matter. Make a contract with yourself to reward yourself for the efforts you make as well as the progress you make toward achieving your goal. When you are playing your very best, there is a certain inner satisfaction that is difficult to describe or characterize. The late humanistic psychologist Abraham Maslow referred to these magic moments as *peak experiences*. At these times we feel physically free, the body and mind are in harmony, and it seems that our execution is without flaw. The experience is sheer pleasure, and not just in terms of satisfaction with results—it simply feels good. These moments are as rare in sport as they are in life, but they are worth the effort put forth in practice and competitions. Success is setting out to accomplish something and doing it; along the way, you may find a joy that is much more meaningful than the final score.

SUGGESTED TASK FOR THE LEARNER

1. Visit a professional tackle shop and examine the equipment and other paraphernalia available. Examine the charts giving information about arrow spine.

2. Most shops have a small shooting area. Ask to try some of the equipment and discuss your needs with the salesperson.

3. Conduct the bare-arrow test with the equipment the school has provided for your use. What would have to be done to tune the bow for your needs?

4. Write out a checklist for yourself. Mentally rehearse when you are away from the range.

5. Chart where your arrows land at different distances. Are the same deviations evident? Determine the probable cause and write out a plan needed for correction.

6. Make yourself a finger sling and practice using it over several shooting sessions. How are the groupings—improved, or about the same?

7. After you have had some shooting experience, experiment with stance and weight distribution. Describe any differences in the results to a fellow student.

8. Draw a bow with a standard handle and one that has a contoured grip. Describe any differences you experience.

9. Construct a chart or checklist for use in analyzing shooting form. Using your checklist, observe a fellow student's performance; locate any difficulties and write out suggestions for improvement.

10. Have someone take slow-motion pictures of your shooting form. Analyze yourself and write out a plan for self-improvement.

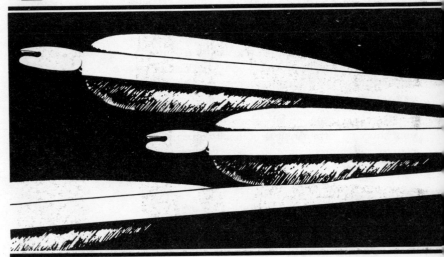

ARCHERY SPORTS AND GAMES

Fundamental archery skills can be applied in a variety of sports and games. Target archery, field archery, indoor archery, clout shooting, and flight shooting are conducted as athletic contests. The National Archery Association (NAA) provides information on the layout of shooting ranges, tournament rules, championship rounds, clout, team, cross bow, and flight shooting. Field archery has a separate governing body. Hunting and fishing are mainly recreational activities. A number of games and novelty shoots have been developed. Some of these games simulate conditions encountered in hunting, others are variations of existing games. All are fun and provide an opportunity to improve skill in shooting.

The emphasis in this chapter is on target archery, since this is the form of the sport most often taught in schools and colleges. Once the basics of shooting are mastered, the opportunity for their application is limited only by the imagination and interest of the shooter.

CONVENTIONAL TARGET ARCHERY

Target archery is conducted on a shooting range where the participants send arrows into a standard five-color target. Each archer shoots a given number of arrows from certain designated distances according to a set procedure. Knowledge of terminology, scoring, rules, and tournament procedure are necessary for participation. Each sport has its own unique vocabulary. Similar terms may be used in more than one form of the sport but may have different meanings. The list below pertains to conventional target archery.

Terminology

End

Usually six arrows shot consecutively or in two groups of three. Some rounds consist of five arrow ends.

Field captain or Lady paramount

The presiding official in charge of a tournament.

Hit

An arrow that lands within the scoring area on the target.

Penetration

An arrow imbedded in the target so that it is not visible on the face or one that passes completely through the target.

Petticoat

The edge of the target beyond the outside ring. An arrow striking this area does not score or count as a hit.

Range

The distance to be shot; the shooting area; an indoor or outdoor archery ground.

Rebound

An arrow that bounces off the scoring area of the target.

Round

A term used to describe a given number of arrows or ends shot at a designated distance or distances.

Target captain

The archer in charge of each target.

Scoring

Target archery rounds are shot at a regulation 48″ target face unless otherwise specified. Target faces are divided into five concentric rings and scored from the center outward. The middle, or gold, counts nine points, the red seven points, the blue five points, the black three points, and the white one point. For international competition, each of the rings is divided in half and the top score is ten so that the gold counts ten and nine; the red eight and seven; the blue six and five; the black four and three; and the white two and one.

An arrow cutting the fine line dividing two colors is scored as the higher value. Rebounds or penetrations, if witnessed, receive seven points unless all arrow holes have been marked and the point of impact can be ascertained. Arrows are pulled from the scoring face by the target captain and recorded on the score sheet with the highest numerical value first and the lowest last. A sample score card for a Columbia Round is shown in Figure. 7.1. In the American Round the archers each shoot 30 arrows at 60, 50, and 40 yards. In the Columbia Round the archers each shoot 24 arrows at 50, 40, and 30 yards. It is important to keep a record of hits in case of a tie. If scores are tied at the end of competition, the winner is the archer with the greatest number of hits.

Tournament Shooting

In tournament shooting, the archers are usually assigned to targets in the order in which they register. After the first round or the first half of a single round, the archers are reassigned so that those with the highest scores are placed on the first target, next highest on the second target and so on. No more than five and preferably only four people are assigned to a given target. Each of the archers has specific duties and responsibilities in a tournament.

ARCHERY SCORE							Hits	Score
Name	J. SMITH							
Date	MAY 3			198 0				
Yds	7	5	3	1	0	0	4	16
50	9	7	7	5	1	0	5	29
	7	7	5	3	3	1	6	26
	9	9	7	3	0	0	4	28
Percentage						Total	19	99
Yds	7	5	1	0	0	0	3	13
40	9	5	3	3	1	0	5	21
	9	9	7	5	5	3	6	38
	9	9	7	7	3	1	6	36
Percentage						Total	20	108
Yds	7	7	7	5	1	1	6	28
30	9	7	7	5	3	3	6	34
	9	9	9	9	5	1	6	42
	9	9	9	7	7	5	6	46
Percentage						Total	24	150
Grand Total						Total	63	357
TEAM TOTAL								

Figure 7.1
Score card.

Target captain. The first person listed on the score sheet acts as the target captain. Before the arrows are withdrawn and scored, he examines the target to determine whether there are any questionable arrows. If he cannot make a decision on an arrow, the field captain or lady paramount is called. Once the face of the target has been checked, the target captain pulls the arrows for each archer separately, calling the values as he does so.

Scorers. The second two people on the score sheet are designated as the scorers. They record the scores as called by the target captain and add the totals. Two scorers are used to avoid mistakes, and they check with one another after each end and each distance round.

Retrievers. The remaining shooters are assigned to retrieve all arrows which miss the target.

Field captain or Lady paramount. The presiding official in a tournament signals the start and finish of each end of shooting. Any problems or scoring decisions that cannot be resolved by the target captain are referred to this official.

Split ends are customary in most large tournaments. A split end consists of the first two archers shooting three arrows each, followed by the second group of two or three archers shooting the same. The first two shooters then shoot their last three arrows, followed by the second group.

Rules for Competition and Safety

Rules are necessary for any sport. Some safety rules have already been presented in Chapter 5, and these should be reviewed. Here are some basic competition rules and some additional safety procedures:

1. All archers shoot from and straddle a common shooting line.

2. Arrows are nocked after the signal to shoot is given.

3. Only five or six arrows may be legally shot; if more are shot, only the lowest are scored.

4. Arrows are considered shot if they fall from the bow and cannot be reached with the aid of the bow while standing on the shooting line.

5. After shooting an end, step back from the shooting line until the signal to retrieve is given. Courtesy dictates that you remain on the line until others on your target have completed their end.

6. Arrows must remain in the target until withdrawn by the target captain.

7. Retrieve arrows only on the appropriate signal.

8. The longest-distance round is shot first, the second-longest next, and so forth.

9. If scores are tied, the archer with the most number of hits is the winner.

10. No practice is permitted between the distances which constitute a round once the tournament is underway. All practice ends must be shot prior to the start of shooting for score.

11. Arrows must have distinctive markings or crests so that the individual archer's arrows are easily identified.

12. All bows, except a cross bow, are legal for tournament competition. Compound bows are not legal for some types of tournaments.

13. Only a legal sight attached to the bow may be used.

14. Point-of-aim markers may not be placed more than 6″ above the ground.

15. Scores are recorded from high to low. Misses or arrows landing outside the scoring face are indicated with a zero.

Common Tournament Rounds

The National Archery Association classifies archers by age and sex for purposes of competition. Beginners are 11 years and younger, juniors are 12 to 14, intermediates 15 to 17, and adults 18 and older. Competitive rounds are available for each classification. Table 3 summarizes some of the more common rounds of interest to students at the college level.

FITA Rounds

The Fédération Internationale de Tir à l'Arc (FITA) is the organization concerned with establishing rules and standards for world championship meets. The body is also known as the Federation for International Target Archery or the International Archery Federation. Inclusion of archery in the Olympics has encouraged the practice of FITA rounds. Collegiate archers should become familiar with the rules and scoring used in international competition. The FITA championship rounds are summarized in Table 4.

Team Competition

Many schools and clubs have team competitions. A team usually consists of four members, but the number can vary. In competition, any number may form a team, provided that the teams competing have an equal number of participants. Clubs often shoot against one another and average the scores of all shooters to determine the winner. Team rounds suggested by the NAA consist of 96 arrows at 60 yards for men and 96 arrows at 50 yards for women.

TABLE 3
Common Target Rounds

Round	Ends	Distance	Arrows Per End	Total	Maximum Score	Commonly Shot By
American	5	60 yards	6	90 arrows	810	Men, women
	5	50 yards	6	15 ends		Intermediates
	5	40 yards	6			
Columbia	4	50 yards	6	72 arrows	748	Women; inter-
	4	40 yards	6	12 ends		mediate and
	4	30 yards	6			junior girls;
						high school and
						college students
Collegiate 600	4	50 meters	5	60 arrows	600*	College students
	4	40 meters	5	12 ends		
	4	30 meters	5			
Easton 600	4	60 meters	5	60 arrows	600*	Men, women
	4	50 meters	5	12 ends		
	4	40 meters	5			
NAA 900	5	50 meters	6	90 arrows	900*	Men, women
(championship	5	40 meters	6	15 ends		
round)	5	30 meters	6			

*These rounds use ten-ring (ten-point scoring) targets

The National Archery Association promotes competition at the college and university level. Meets are conducted on a shoulder-to-shoulder basis as well as by mail or telegram. In shoulder-to-shoulder competition, all shooters are present on the same range. In mail or telegraphic shoots, the archers compete on their home range and the scores are forwarded to the tournament chairman or host school. The types of rounds shot vary

TABLE 4
FITA Championship Rounds

Round	Ends	Distance	Arrows (6 per end)	Target	Maximum Score
Men's FITA	6	90 meters (98.4 yards)	144 arrows 24 ends	122 cm.	1,440
	6	70 meters (76.6 yards)		122 cm.	
	*6	50 meters (54.7 yards)		80 cm.	
	*6	30 meters (32.8 yards)		80 cm.	

*Makes a short FITA for men or women.

Round	Ends	Distance	Arrows (6 per end)	Target	Maximum Score
Women's FITA	6	70 meters (76.6 yards)	144 arrows 24 ends	122 cm.	1,440
	6	60 meters (65.6 yards)		122 cm.	
	6	50 meters (54.7 yards)		80 cm.	
	6	30 meters (32.8 yards)		80 cm.	

NOTE: All rounds on ten-ring target; FITA rules apply.

with the tournament. Members of the College Division of the National Archery Association (NAACD), which governs college and university competition, have worked hard to promote archery and make it part of the general collegiate athletic program. Hopefully, competition at this level will provide more and better-qualified archers for future international and Olympic events.

Modern Target Archery

The upswing of interest in archery as a competitive sport has led to the development of a number of

TABLE 5
Newer Competitive Rounds

Round	Ends	Distance	Arrows (5 per End)	Total	Scoring & Target	Maximum Score
Scot	12	20 yards	60	60 arrows 12 ends	5-4-3-2-1 25″ Black and gray	300
Professional	12	20 yards	60	60 arrows 12 ends	5-4-3-2-1 16″ Black, P.A.A.	300
Sectional	12	30 yards	60	60 arrows 12 ends	5-4-3-2-1 36″ Four Color	300
Conference	4	50 yards	20	60 arrows 12 ends	5-4-3-2-1 48″ Four Color	300
	4	40 yards	20			
	4	30 yards	20			
Grand American	4	60 yards	20	60 arrows 12 ends	5-4-3-2-1 48″ Four Color	300
	4	50 yards	20			
	4	40 yards	20			

variations in conventional target archery. Many new competitive rounds have been initiated, designed to appeal to archers of all levels of ability; many can be used equally well indoors and outdoors. Some of the new rounds are adaptations or modifications of field archery rounds, and require the archer to shoot from several distances at targets varying in size and design. Others use the more conventional five-color target but the size is smaller and scoring starts with a high of five points and goes to a low of one point. All of the rounds are based on a perfect score of 300, and only five arrows constitute an end. The perfect 300 resembles the scores associated with bowling. The idea of one top score for several different rounds is useful since it enables people to interpret the score in relation to a set standard. A number of the newer rounds are outlined in Table 5.

INDOOR ARCHERY LANES

Indoor archery lanes are a relatively new innovation. The advent of the automated target has been a boon to the serious archer and has extended the opportunity for participation to many others. Archery has traditionally been an outdoor sport. This meant that the shooter had to have sufficient free time during daylight hours to practice and compete. Indoor archery is now available at all hours, and even seasonal changes do not affect its operation.

Archery lanes are operated in a manner similar to bowling lanes. The house has the necessary equipment available, and the archer pays an hourly rate for use of the facilities. Most operators provide an instructor to help beginners and coach more advanced performers. The archer shoots at a target which moves automatically to any distance he selects. Arrows are retrieved by pressing a button on the console, causing the target to move up to the shooting line. Once the target has reached the shooter, he scores his hits and removes his arrows. Most archery centers have leagues which operate during the evening hours. The leagues are often handicapped, and it is not unusual to have teams composed of all men, all women, and couples shooting against one another. Archery enthusiasts are hopeful that their sport will become as popular as bowling and golf, and feel that the automated lanes will foster the growth and development of this sport.

FIELD ARCHERY

Interest in field archery has grown tremendously since the first official tournament held in 1946. The National Field Archery Association (NFAA) is the governing organization, providing information on course construction, rules interpretation, formation of clubs, and sponsorship of tournaments. Field archery tournaments are conducted in both freestyle (sight shooters) and bare-bow (instinctive shooters) classifications.

The main difference between target and field archery is the structure of the shooting range. Both sports involve shooting at stationary targets, but in field archery the range is larger and involves a variety of terrain. The archer moves from one shooting station to another, often through woods and brush, and shoots at special field faces. The distances shot differ at each target, and some stations require shots from more than one position. The size of the target faces used range from 12" to 24" depending on the distance shot. An end in field archery consists of four arrows. The standard field-target face has two concentric circles with an aiming spot in the center. A hit in the inner circle scores five points and one in the outer circle, three. This exciting and challenging sport places many demands on the archer; it is easy to see why this form of archery has become so popular over the last several years.

CLOUT SHOOTING

Clout shooting is a form of competition sanctioned by the NAA but it is also engaged in as a "fun" activity. Distances used in clout rounds vary with the archer's shooting classification. Women shoot from a distance of 120 or 140 yards. Men are placed 180 yards from the target. The clout target resembles that used for conventional target archery except that it is 48' in diameter and laid out on the ground. The archer sends his arrows high into the air toward a flag marking the center of the target. A clout round consists of 36 arrows (6 ends) and is scored in the same manner as the conventional five-color target.

FLIGHT SHOOTING

The basic idea in flight shooting is to send an arrow the maximum distance possible. Competitors are restricted to certain categories authorized by the NAA. Each division is further classified by weight and type of bow. Each classification has an unlimited weight competition and a foot-bow competition. The foot bow is a bow with an extremely heavy draw weight that is drawn with both hands while braced against the archer's feet. Flight shooting has limited appeal, but its enthusiasts are dedicated. It is not unusual for an adherent of the sport to spend months designing and constructing a flight shooting bow in an effort to make that one perfect shot.

HUNTING

Hunting is different from competitive archery in many ways. Every hunter must be familiar with the basics of shooting but must also be able to adjust his tackle and technique for different game. Hunting arrows are designed to accommodate a larger, heavier point and, usually, longer feathers. Bow hunting is a very specialized form of archery and requires much more than the ability to handle a bow and arrow competently. The hunter must employ other skills and be familiar with the habits of the game he is stalking. Students concerned with the hunting aspect of archery are urged to master the fundamentals of shooting and practice with the equipment they intend to use. Although there are several informative books on the sport of bow hunting, the best means to learn is to participate with an experienced bow hunter.

GAMES AND NOVELTY SHOOTS

Archery games can be played on the range, in the backyard, or almost any convenient, safe area. The games and novelty shoots included here present unique challenges to the archer. All can be a source of fun and enjoyment while helping to perfect shooting skill.

Archery Golf. Archery golf is played on a regulation golf course or on any large outdoor area. The rules are basically the same as those used for playing golf. The "cup" consists of a ball placed on a stand which the archer must hit to complete the hole. When the game is played on a regulation course, a par of one stroke less than that designated for the golfer is used. Archery golf combines elements of the clout and target techniques and requires good depth perception and accuracy.

Roving Archery. Archers move about an area in groups of three or four and pick targets at random. The target might be a piece of paper, a bush, a clump of grass, or the like. Each archer shoots one arrow at the target selected. The shooter who hits the target or comes closest receives a point and has the privilege of determining the next target.

Wand Shooting. The target is made of soft wood, 2″ wide and 6′ high. Women shoot 36 arrows at 60 yards. Men shoot 36 arrows at 100 yards. The wood is usually placed over a butt so that misses are stopped immediately. Arrows rebounding from the wand are scored as hits. Wand shooting is a very old archery game and was played in England as early as the sixteenth century.

Pope Young Round. This is a round for speed and accuracy. Six shooting stations are set up. Six targets are arranged from 20 to 80 yards. Six ends constitute a round. Six arrows are shot from one station in 45 seconds. Each arrow is shot at a different target. After each end is scored, the archers move to another station in a rotating order. One point is scored per hit. Animal faces may be used as targets. *(Note: This round should only be used by archers who have had experience and who shoot with sights or instinctively.)*

Tic-Tac-Toe. Nine balloons are arranged on the target in lines of three across and three down. Archers on each target form a file. At the signal to shoot, the first archer shoots one arrow and goes to the end of the line. Each succeeding player repeats the action. The first team to break three balloons in any straight line wins. The distance from the target can vary, but 20 yards seems to offer sufficient challenge for the average person. As a point of safety, no one is allowed to take an arrow from the quiver until on the shooting line.

Still-Hunting the Buck. A burlap deer is constructed with two ovals marking its vitals, the heart being inside the larger oval. One player hides the deer, leaving a trail of kernels of corn, dropping one every yard. After ten minutes the hunters surge forth. The first to sight the deer calls, "Deer." He shoots from that point. If he misses in three tries, the others shoot one arrow each. If all miss, they take five steps and shoot again. This continues until they are 10 yards from the deer, or until it is hit; in which case further shooting is done from the spot where the hit was made. A shot in the heart scores ten and ends the hunt. A shot in the large oval scores five. A hit outside the oval scores two. If all shoot 10 yards from the deer without a hit, the hider scores 25 and the deer is hidden again. The hunter with the highest score wins.

Bow Bird Shooting. Flu-flu arrows and bow-bird targets are needed for this game. Both items can be purchased commercially. If flu-flu arrows are not available, reasonably satisfactory ones can be made by using the "feathers" of plastic badminton birds. The heads of the plastic shuttlecocks often wear out and the entire bird is discarded. To convert a regular target arrow into a flu-flu arrow, remove the plastic part of the shuttlecock and cut lines in the base so that it will slide up the shaft of the arrow close to the feathers. A small-game blunt is attached to the point of the arrow for balance. These arrows will not fly as true as those that are specially made, but prove quite satisfactory for this game. Bow-bird targets can be constructed by taping together circular disks cut out of heavy cardboard. Plastic "flying saucers" can also be used for targets.

The game is usually played as a team activity. The archers are lined up behind one another with a thrower to one side (hidden from view if possible). A member of each team steps to the line. When each has his arrow nocked, the range captain calls, "Pull." The thrower can throw the bird at any time within 20 seconds after the call and at any angle or elevation. Each team member gets at least three shots. Hits count for score and the high team total wins. A target distance of about 10 yards in front of the shooting line seems to be satisfactory for this game.

Other Games. There are a great many other games that can be played with the use of the bow and arrow. Archers can shoot at targets from different positions such as kneeling, standing on one leg, or left-handed. The object of Archery Monopoly is to get all arrows in one color, and, if successful, the shooter gets to keep all of the arrows in that color. The target can also be scored backward so that the white ring is high and the gold ring low. Stuffed-rabbit hunts, a number of balloon events, and shoots that use specially constructed target faces are additional activities. The list is almost endless and is a credit to the creativity of the archery enthusiast.

SUGGESTED TASKS FOR THE LEARNER

1. Determine the location of all archery clubs and ranges in the area surrounding your school and permanent residence.

2. Arrange to observe an archery tournament in progress. List the procedures you observe regarding safety, dress of the participants, the method of scoring, the duties of the archers, the general conduct of the participants, and so forth..

3. Visit an indoor archery lane if there is one in your area.

4. Determine how many schools and colleges in your vicinity have archery teams, and the extent of their activity.

5. Indicate how you would go about finding information on rules, course layouts, and tournament procedure for the various competitive archery sports.

6. Make up a special archery round that is suitable for use at your institution.

7. Determine a means of establishing handicaps for equalizing competition among archers of varying levels of ability.

8. Make up a game or novelty shoot that can be played by members of your class.

8

POINTING UP PROGRESS

E arlier in this book, it was maintained that the learner must do his own learning. An instructor helps shorten the learning time by eliminating much of the trial and error, but it is still necessary to apply the instructor's suggestions to the performance. Archery activity provides immediate feedback information. Knowledge of results helps to point up progress and serves to reinforce learning. Quantitative archery scores provide information about level of ability and are a meaningful indication of learning. A systematic means of recording progress helps determine the exact amount of improvement and denotes areas in need of attention.

Several means of analyzing and evaluating shooting ability are presented in this chapter. The list of suggested tasks for the learner, included at the end of each of the preceding chapters, also contributes to evaluation and reinforcement of learning.

ANALYSIS OF FORM AND GENERAL KNOWLEDGE

Checklists and rating sheets are useful for self-appraisal as well as for evaluation by another person. The ratings effectively isolate individual difficulties and aid in determining the nature of the

TASK	COMMENTS
1. Brace bow correctly	
2. Nock arrow correctly	
3. Grip in V, wrist aligned	
4. Hold bown arm in slightly flexed position with shoulder down	
5. Draw with upper back, shoulder and upper arm muscles	
6. Use three fingers as hooks on string	
7. Use exactly the same foot position and weight distribution	
8. Draw to exactly the same anchor and distance	
9. Hold long enough to aim	
10. Follow through after release	
11. Use a sight correctly	
12. Keep a score sheet	
13. Analyze form and correct for the errors	
14. Group arrows on the target	
15. Retrieve arrows correctly	

Figure 8.1 *Example of a self-checklist.*

Figure 8.2 *Archery rating sheet. (See page 115.)*

experiences necessary to remedy the problems. See Figure 8.1 for sample self-checklist and Figure 8.2 for an archery rating sheet.

DIRECTIONS: Place the dates you checked each item in the columns to the left. Enter the date you *know* you mastered each task in the right-hand column.

Photographs and Pictures. Many schools now own portable television-taping machines. These can provide an immediate picture of the performance and

NAME:	DATE:	/	/	/	/	COMMENTS
S	Feet not placed consistently					
T	Weight uneven					
A	Body incorrectly aligned					
N						
C						
E						
N	Nocking point inconsistent					
O	Position of fingers incorrect					
C						
K						
D	Pressure on arrow nock					
R	String fingers and arm used					
A	Bow wrist flexed or hyperextended					
W	Draw elbow below wrist of drawing hand					
	Bow canted					
	Bow elbow not rotated out					
	Bow shoulder hunched					
	Head moves or tilts					
	Body moves					
AIM	Incorrect eye used					
N	Bow arm unsteady					
C	Anchor inconsistent					
H	No hold or aim apparent					
O						
R						
R	Body moves					
E	Bow arm moves					
L	String arm and hand moves incorrectly					
E						
A						
S						
E						
HOLD	No follow-through					

GROUPING WHILE RATED
1 | 2 | 3 | 4

RATED BY:
1.
2.
3.
4.

are extremely beneficial in analyzing form. Graph-check photographs aid in analysis and furnish a permanent visual record of individual form. (See Figure 8.3.) Moving pictures and still photographs also supply a means of checking technique and, if taken often enough, serve as a record of progress. For best results, pictures should be used in conjunction with the charts previously indicated.

SCORE AND ACCURACY ANALYSIS

Scores, plotted on a graph or compared with established standards, are another means of ascertaining individual development. The use of a card or form to

Figure 8.3 *Example of a graph-check photograph. What suggestions can you make to improve the form?*

locate hits on, or in the area of, the target helps in determining progress and points to areas in need of practice.

Accuracy-Analysis Chart. The position of each arrow is marked with a dot for each end of shooting at each distance. If the cards are properly dated and filed, progress, or lack of it, is clearly evident. The record also helps indicate the existence of a faulty arrow in the set. If arrows are numbered or individuals identified in some manner, the code for the arrow is entered in the card in the appropriate space. Faulty or damaged arrows are easily located after a few ends. See Figure 8.4 for an example of an accuracy-analysis chart.

Profile Chart. Profile charts, plotted on graph paper for selected rounds or distances, provide visual evidence of progress. The chart often has valleys and peaks, but improvement should be demonstrated over an extended period. Scores that dip below the average over several shooting sessions indicate the need to look for errors in form or other learning problems.

Percentiles. Many schools keep records of scores made by students in archery classes over a period of years. Tables are constructed and posted for reference. Individual progress and achievement is determined by checking personal scores against the chart. If the score falls at the sixtieth percentile, it means that the individual scored better than 60 percent of the students who were enrolled in a similar class. Checking percentiles for each complete round or for each distance shot also provides a meaningful record of improvement. If at the beginning of the course scores are at the tenth percentile and halfway through have moved to the fortieth, the implication is clearly evident.

Score Comparison. Other means of assessing progress are use of standardized achievement charts and contrasting personal achievement with championship level performance. Table 6 shows a proficiency chart which was established based on scores for several beginning archery classes over a five-year period. The letter grade does not represent the grade for the course, as criteria in addition to proficiency are used to calculate the final grade. Scores between 625 and 675 would be considered very good for a typical college student shooting an American round. However, championship-level collegiate women exceed 720 for this round, while men total 785 and better. Championship form in the Easton 600 has women averaging 540 and men about 560. Scores beyond 1,200 have been recorded for women collegiate champions in the FITA round; similar totals have been recorded for the men's FITA round,

Name _____

Date _____ Card No. _____

Distance Shot _____ End No. _____ Distance Shot _____ End No. _____

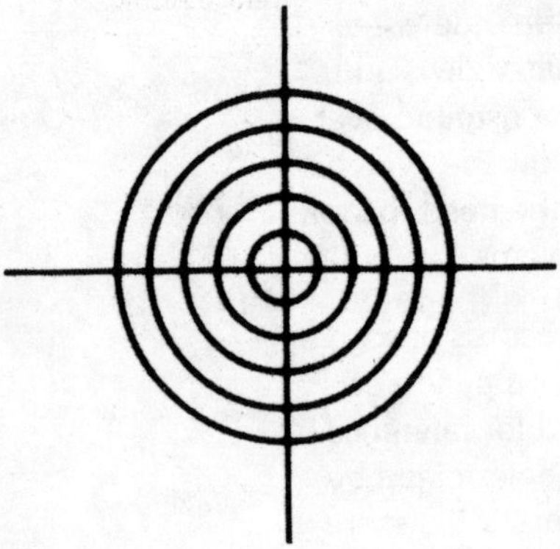

Comment: 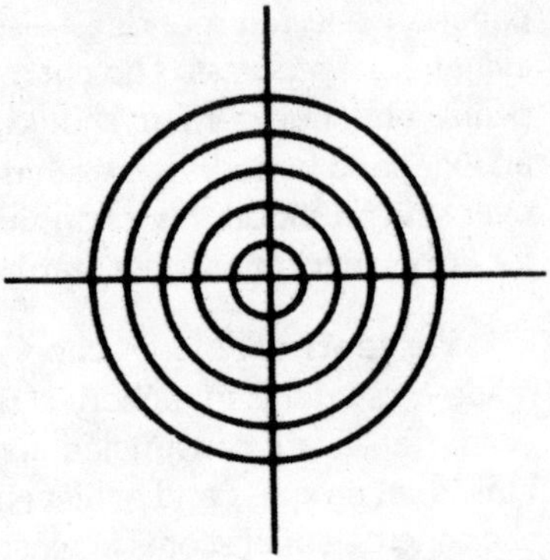   Comment:

Distance Shot _____ End No. _____ Distance Shot _____ End No. _____

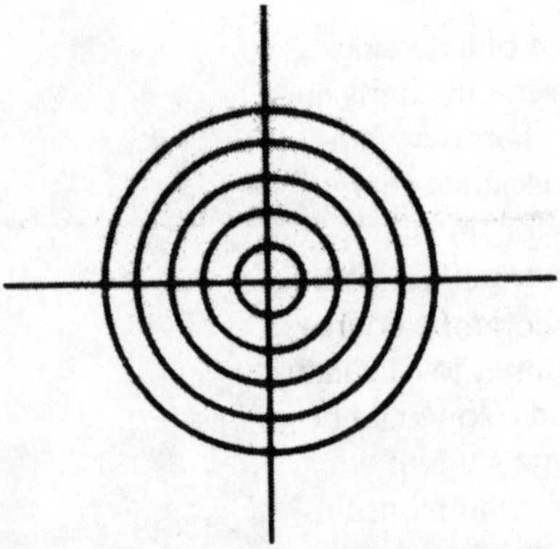

Comment: 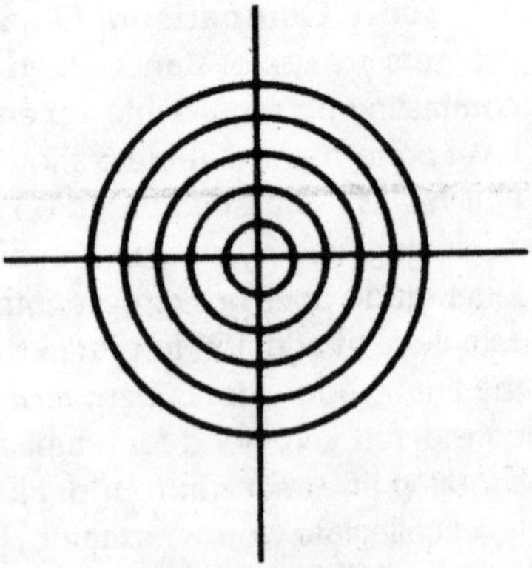   Comment:

Figure 8.4 Accuracy-analysis chart.

TABLE 6

Beginning Archery Columbia Round Standards

Level (Grade)	MEN Range	Average Arrow
1 (A+)	420+	5.83+
2 (A)	408 - 419	5.66 - 5.82
3 (A−)	396 - 407	5.50 - 5.65
4 (B+)	378 - 395	5.25 - 5.49
5 (B)	360 - 377	5.00 - 5.24
6 (B−)	342 - 359	4.75 - 4.99
7 (C+)	306 - 341	4.25 - 4.74
8 (C)	270 - 305	3.75 - 4.24
9 (C−)	234 - 269	3.25 - 3.74
10 (D+)	216 - 233	3.00 - 3.24
11 (D)	204 - 215	2.83 - 2.99
12 (D−)	180 - 203	2.50 - 2.82

Level (Grade)	WOMEN Range	Average Arrow
1 (A+)	384+	5.33+
2 (A)	372 - 383	5.17 - 5.32
3 (A−)	360 - 371	5.00 - 5.16
4 (B+)	342 - 359	4.75 - 4.99
5 (B)	324 - 341	4.50 - 4.74
6 (B−)	306 - 323	4.25 - 4.49
7 (C+)	270 - 305	3.73 - 4.24
8 (C)	234 - 269	3.25 - 3.74
9 (C−)	198 - 233	2.75 - 3.24
10 (D+)	180 - 197	2.50 - 2.74
11 (D)	162 - 179	2.25 - 2.49
12 (D−)	144 - 161	2.00 - 2.24

which utilizes longer distances. A FITA score of 1,050 or more for either men or women is considered championship-level performance.

INDIVIDUAL PROGRAMS

Each learner learns at his own rate. This must be kept in mind as achievement is measured. Each person needs to establish his own goal and work out a plan for reaching it. The devices indicated previously are helpful in implementing progress toward the objective, but the objective must clearly be the intent of the learner.

Programs can be quantitative (a score or number), qualitative (how well), or both. One idea for designing an individual program at different levels is presented in Figure 8.5. Each learner is urged to think through all the tasks involved in learning to handle a bow and arrow competently, and to design his own program for accomplishing them.

Learning is a process as well as a product. The more you, the student, are involved in the learning process, the more meaningful and satisfying the experience becomes. The end product may be a certain skill level in shooting a bow and arrow, but in the process you may also discover a new image of yourself. *Archery is a means to an end—an end in itself.*

INDIVIDUAL PROGRAM NO. _____

Name _____

TASK: Shoot _____ arrows or _____ ends from a distance of _____ yards

LEVELS	DESCRIPTION	A	B	COMMENTS/REACTIONS
Level 1	Half of all arrows shot, each end, hit scoring area			
Level 2	All arrows shot, each end, hit scoring area			
Level 3	All arrows shot hit on or inside the blue ring			
Level 4	Score not less than _____ for each end shot with all arrows hitting within scoring area			

DIRECTIONS: In column A record the date you were *first* able to accomplish the task at the given level. In column B put the date you were able to accomplish the task on _____ consecutive days of shooting.

Figure 8.5 *Example of individual program design — multi-level.*

SUGGESTED READINGS

Archery.
    Palm Springs CA: National Field Archery Association
Archery World.
    Boyertown, PA: Archery Associates, Inc.
Baiek, Patricia, and others *Instructor's Manual.*
    Lancaster, PA: National Archery Association, 1976.
Bow and Arrow.
    Covina, CA: Gallant Publishing.

Burke, Edmund H. *Archery Handbook*.
  Greenwich, CT: Fawcett Publications, 1954.
Burke, Edmund H. *Field and Target Archery*.
  Greenwich, CT: Fawcett Publications, 1961.
Burke, Edmund H. *The History of Archery*.
  New York: Morrow, 1957.
Division for Girls' and Women's Sports. *Archery-Riding Guide*.
  Washington, DC: AAHPER.
Elmer, Robert P. *Target Archery*.
  New York: Knopf, 1946.
Forbes, Thomas A. *New Guide to Better Archery*.
  Harrisburg, PA: Stackpole, 1960.
Haugen, Arnold O., and Metcalf, Harland G., *Field Archery and Bowhunting*.
  New York: Ronald Press, 1968.
Herrigel, Eugen. *Zen in the Art of Archery*.
  New York: McGraw-Hill, 1964.
Honda, Shig, and others. *Archery*.
  Boston: Allyn Bacon, 1975.
Houghman, Paul C. *The Encyclopedia of Archery*.
  New York: Barnes, 1957.
Jaeger, Eloise. *Archery Instructor's Guide*.
  Chicago: The Athletic Institute, 1960.
Keaggy, David J., Sr. *Power Archery*.
  Riderwood, MD: *Archery World Magazine*, 1964.
Klann, Margaret L. *Target Archery*.
  Menlo Park, CA: Addison-Wesley, 1970.
Love, Albert J. *Field Archery Technique*.
  Corpus Christi, TX: Dotson, 1956.
McKinney, Wayne C. *Archery*.
  Dubuque, IA: William C. Brown, 1975.
National Archery Association. *The Archer's Handbook*.
  Lancaster, PA: National Archery Association, 1974.
Niemeyer, Roy K., and Zabik, Roger M. *Beginning Archery*.
  Belmont, CA: Wadsworth, 1978.
Pearson, Ben. *Archery for Everyone*.
  Pine Bluff, AR: Ben Pearson, Inc.
Pszczoła, Lorraine. *Archery*.
  Philadelphia: Saunders, 1976.
Roberts, Daniel. *Archery for All*.
  North Vancouver, BC: David and Charles, 1976.
Young, Dick. *Let's Raise Our Score*.
  Los Angeles: American Offset Printers, 1969.

PERFORMANCE CHECK LIST

HOW TO USE THE EVALUATION FORMS

The forms which follow were designed to be used in a variety of instructional settings. Preplanning and organization are necessary for these devices to be used as effectively as possible. The purpose of evaluation is for gauging how well the course objectives are accomplished. That is, evaluation will indicate the progress and the extent to which learning has occurred.

Although the learner *must do his own learning*, the teacher's role is to guide and to direct learning experiences and to provide for appropriate measurement procedures. The charts which follow have been constructed to place primary responsibility on the individual student for estimating progress and indicating areas which need work. It may not be either necessary or desirable to use all the materials provided here in a given teaching-learning situation. The instructor and the learner should work together to select the materials most appropriate for the course.

It must be remembered that sufficient time for practice and study must be provided if the individual is to perfect his skills as well as develop understanding. The time available may not be adequate for *all* learners to demonstrate acceptable levels of skill performance. The instructor may wish to supplement the evaluation devices with a written test covering analysis of performance, procedures, and rules. The written test provides an opportunity for the learner to demonstrate his knowledge and understanding of the sport even though his actual skill might be less than desired. Final evaluation for grading purposes should take into account a number of variables which may have an influence on individual performance.

ARCHERY RATING SHEET

Name _____ Class _____

To the learner: Work with another learner and have him observe you shoot a minimum of 2 and preferably 4 ends. The observer should check areas you need to work on to improve your performance. After you have discussed the evaluation with the rater, check your textbook and write suggested corrections on the reverse side. Turn the form in to the instructor when specified.

LEARNER   **STANCE**   INSTRUCTOR

_____   Feet not placed consistently   _____

_____   Weight uneven   _____

_____   Body incorrectly aligned   _____

NOCK

_____   Nocking point inconsistent   _____

_____   Position of fingers incorrect   _____

DRAW

_____   Pressure on arrow nock   _____

_____   String fingers and arm used   _____

_____   Bow wrist flexed or hyperextended   _____

_____   Draw elbow below wrist of drawing hand   _____

_____   Bow canted   _____

_____   Bow elbow not rotated out   _____

_____   Bow shoulder hunched   _____

_____   Head moves or tilts   _____

_____   Body moves   _____

AIM ANCHOR

_____   Incorrect eye used   _____

_____   Bow arm unsteady   _____

_____   Anchor inconsistent   _____

_____   No hold or aim apparent   _____

RELEASE

_____   Body moves   _____

_____   Bow arm moves   _____

_____   String arm and hand moves incorrectly   _____

HOLD

_____   No follow-through   _____

ACCURACY ANALYSIS FORM

NAME _____ CLASS _____

To the learner: After taking an end or two to "sight in" for the distance, record where each of your arrows strikes (or misses) the target for each end by placing a dot (•) or an X in the approximate area. Comment on the grouping and make suggestions for corrections, if necessary. NOTE — if arrows are numbered, record number of each arrow at spot.

LEARNER   Distance Shot _____ End No. _____   INSTRUCTOR

LEARNER   Distance Shot _____ End No. _____   INSTRUCTOR

LEARNER   Distance Shot _____ End No. _____   INSTRUCTOR

ACCURACY ANALYSIS FORM

NAME _____ CLASS _____

To the learner: After taking an end or two to "sight in" for the distance, record where each of your arrows strikes (or misses) the target for each end by placing a dot (•) or an X in the approximate area. Comment on the grouping and make suggestions for corrections, if necessary. NOTE — if arrows are numbered, record number of each arrow at spot.

LEARNER   Distance Shot _____ End No. _____   INSTRUCTOR

LEARNER   Distance Shot _____ End No. _____   INSTRUCTOR

LEARNER   Distance Shot _____ End No. _____   INSTRUCTOR

INDIVIDUAL TASK FORM

NAME _____ CLASS _____

To the learner: Fill in the information relating to the number of ends or arrows selected for the program and the distance. This form is designed for use over a period of time. You may find it easier to complete some of the simpler tasks for several distances before going on to the higher levels. If this is the case, fill out a form for each distance and turn the form in periodically for instructor evaluation and comment. Place date in column when you accomplish task. NOTE: task should not be limited to six arrows or one end.

TASK: Shoot _____ arrows or _____ ends from a distance of _____ yards.

Level	Description	Date	Instructor Comment Initial and Date
1	½ of all arrows shot or ½ the arrows for each end shot hit scoring area		
2	All arrows shot hit scoring area		
3	All arrows shot hit on or inside the black		
4	Score at least 25 points with all arrows in the scoring area		
5	All arrows on target and grouped on or inside the blue target ring		
6	All arrows shot hit on or inside the red		

INDIVIDUAL TASK FORM

NAME _____ CLASS _____

To the learner: Fill in the information relating to the number of ends or arrows selected for the program and the distance. This form is designed for use over a period of time. You may find it easier to complete some of the simpler tasks for several distances before going on to the higher levels. If this is the case, fill out a form for each distance and turn the form in periodically for instructor evaluation and comment. Place date in column when you accomplish task. NOTE: task should not be limited to six arrows or one end.

TASK: Shoot _____ arrows or _____ ends from a distance of _____yards.

Level	Description	Date	Instructor Comment Initial and Date
1	½ of all arrows shot or ½ the arrows for each end shot hit scoring area		
2	All arrows shot hit scoring area		
3	All arrows shot hit on or inside the black		
4	Score at least 25 points with all arrows in the scoring area		
5	All arrows on target and grouped on or inside the blue target ring		
6	All arrows shot hit on or inside the red		

PERCENTILE PERFORMANCE

Name _____ Class _____

To the learner: The instructor will provide you with (or post in some manner) a chart indicating the percentile for a given score for a designated number of arrows at each of several distances. Record your score and the percentile for each distance systematically throughout.

Distance	Date	Score	Percentile	Comment
_____ Yards (Percentile based on _____ arrows or _____ ends)				
_____ Yards (Percentile based on _____ arrows or _____ ends)				
_____ Yards (Percentile based on _____ arrows or _____ ends)				
_____ Yards (Percentile based on _____ arrows or _____ ends)				
_____ Yards (Percentile based on _____ arrows or _____ ends)				

AVERAGE ARROW CHART

Name _____ Class _____

To the learner: At the end of each shooting session add up the number of arrows shot at each distance separately. Divide this into the total score for each distance. This will give you the "average arrow" for the distance. Use a separate chart for each distance and record your average in the appropriate space. Chart the progress by connecting the lines. (See Profile Chart, Chapter 8, for an explanation of possible fluctuations in performance.)

Average arrow at _____ yards.

RANGE	Date	Date	Date	Date	Date	Date	INSTRUCTOR COMMENT
8.0 or Above							
7.8—7.9							
7.6—7.7							
7.4—7.5							
7.2—7.3							
7.0—7.1							
6.8—6.9							
6.6—6.7							
6.4—6.5							
6.2—6.3							
6.0—6.1							
5.8—5.9							
5.6—5.7							
5.4—5.5							
5.2—5.3							
5.0—5.1							
4.8—4.9							
4.6—4.7							
4.4—4.5							
4.2—4.3							
4.0—4.1							
3.8—3.9							
3.6—3.7							
3.4—3.5							
3.2—3.3							
3.0—3.1							
2.8—2.9							
2.6—2.7							
2.4—2.5							
2.2—2.3							
2.0—2.1							
1.9 or Less							

AVERAGE ARROW CHART

NAME _____ CLASS _____

To the learner: At the end of each shooting session add up the number of arrows shot at each distance separately. Divide this into the total score for each distance. This will give you the "average arrow" for the distance. Use a separate chart for each distance and record your average in the appropriate space. Chart the progress by connecting the lines. (See Profile Chart, Chapter 8, for an explanation of possible fluctuations in performance.)

Average arrow at _____ yards.

RANGE	Date	Date	Date	Date	Date	Date	INSTRUCTOR COMMENT
8.0 or Above							
7.8—7.9							
7.6—7.7							
7.4—7.5							
7.2—7.3							
7.0—7.1							
6.8—6.9							
6.6—6.7							
6.4—6.5							
6.2—6.3							
6.0—6.1							
5.8—5.9							
5.6—5.7							
5.4—5.5							
5.2—5.3							
5.0—5.1							
4.8—4.9							
4.6—4.7							
4.4—4.5							
4.2—4.3							
4.0—4.1							
3.8—3.9							
3.6—3.7							
3.4—3.5							
3.2—3.3							
3.0—3.1							
2.8—2.9							
2.6—2.7							
2.4—2.5							
2.2—2.3							
2.0—2.1							
1.9 or Less							

AVERAGE ARROW CHART

NAME _____ CLASS _____

To the learner: At the end of each shooting session add up the number of arrows shot at each distance separately. Divide this into the total score for each distance. This will give you the "average arrow" for the distance. Use a separate chart for each distance and record your average in the appropriate space. Chart the progress by connecting the lines. (See Profile Chart, Chapter 8, for an explanation of possible fluctuations in performance.)

Average arrow at _____ yards.

RANGE	Date	Date	Date	Date	Date	Date	INSTRUCTOR COMMENT
8.0 or Above							
7.8—7.9							
7.6—7.7							
7.4—7.5							
7.2—7.3							
7.0—7.1							
6.8—6.9							
6.6—6.7							
6.4—6.5							
6.2—6.3							
6.0—6.1							
5.8—5.9							
5.6—5.7							
5.4—5.5							
5.2—5.3							
5.0—5.1							
4.8—4.9							
4.6—4.7							
4.4—4.5							
4.2—4.3							
4.0—4.1							
3.8—3.9							
3.6—3.7							
3.4—3.5							
3.2—3.3							
3.0—3.1							
2.8—2.9							
2.6—2.7							
2.4—2.5							
2.2—2.3							
2.0—2.1							
1.9 or Less							

ARCHERY SELF-EVALUATION CHECK LIST

Name _____ Class _____

To the learner: Use the form to indicate your learning progress. When you know you can do the task with consistency, place a check and the date in column 1. The sheet can be turned in to the instructor at specified times. The instructor will initial column 3 if there is agreement with your estimate of ability and will make any necessary comments. Or if the instructor indicates more practice is needed, you can use column 2 for a second check.

STUDENT	TASK	INSTRUCTOR
_____	Brace bow correctly	_____
_____	Nock arrow correctly	_____
_____	Grip in V, wrist aligned	_____
_____	Hold bow arm in slightly flexed position with shoulder down	_____
_____	Draw with upper back, shoulder, and upper arm muscles	_____
_____	Use three fingers as hooks on string	_____
_____	Use exactly same foot position and weight distribution	_____
_____	Draw to exactly the same anchor and distance	_____
_____	Hold long enough to aim	_____
_____	Follow-through after release	_____
_____	Use a sight correctly	_____
_____	Keep a score sheet	_____
_____	Analyze form and correct for the errors	_____
_____	Group arrows on the target	_____
_____	Retrieve arrows correctly	_____
_____	Date turned in	_____
_____	Date all tasks completed	_____